To John Grant

THE
MALT FILE

*The independent guide to single malt
whiskies and their distilleries*

Sláinte

Tasting notes by
John D. Lamond

Background and history by
Robin Tuček

St Andrew's Day, 1992.

D1471541

The
MALT WHISKY
Association

Published 1991 by The Malt Whisky Association
First edition published 1989
Reprinted 1991
©1989 and 1991 Master of Malt Ltd

To Margaret Ballard

Design & illustrations: Sarah Medway
of Lavis Coleman

Printed and bound in Great Britain by
M & A Thomson Litho Ltd
East Kilbride Glasgow Scotland

ISBN 1 870042 01 8

Introduction

The Malt File is intended as a ready reference book for the serious malt whisky drinker. It gives background and tasting notes to those single malt whiskies which are currently available in bottle.

Naturally, some single malts are easier to come by than others; certain of those listed in this book can only be obtained from the more specialised outlets. Some, which were produced by distilleries now closed, are destined to become rare collectors' items.

In a few cases, where we have not been able to obtain a sample for tasting, we have nevertheless included background notes to the distillery entry. Many single malts are marketed at more than one age. In these cases, we have given additional tasting notes where samples have been available to us.

For the purpose of guiding rather than leading the reader, I have assessed the available malts on colour, nose, taste and finish, using terminology which I trust will be accessible to the general reader as well as the connoisseur. I have indicated no preferences or given suggestions as to where when and how the whiskies should be drunk — I think that is entirely up to you.

The purpose of The Malt File is to help you experience and enjoy as many different single malt whiskies as possible. Each of you will find that certain whiskies offer greater enjoyment to your palate than others. So be it. One of the pleasures of single malt whisky is that there will probably be very few that each of us won't want to taste again.

It is a source of continuing wonder and fascination that from such simple ingredients and with a similar process, the great distilleries can produce a range and subtlety of flavour that covers the widest spectrum of taste and style. If you are as fascinated as I am by malt whisky and its history, then this book should aid you on your journey of discovery.

Slainte,

John Lamond
Master of Malt

You take the Highland . . .

No two single malt whiskies are alike. Even malts produced by sister distilleries using the same source of water have their own distinct individuality. But, although single malt whiskies cannot be neatly packaged and parcelled, certain whiskies do have shared characteristics which, although broadly defined, can help to identify a malt's original provenance. For example, some, but not all, Island malts share similarities, as do some Speyside whiskies, particularly those grouped around the river Livet.

The traditional regions are Highland, Lowland, Islay and Campbeltown, although the latters's once numerous distilleries have now dwindled to just two. It is possible also to sub-divide the Highland region into Speyside, Northern Highland, Eastern Highland, Perthshire, and Island (not to be confused with Islay) malts.

Islay malts are the weightiest, most pungent and most heavily peated, and are therefore generally the easiest to identify. These malts take their characteristics both from the peat used to dry the barley and their closeness to the sea. These factors give them what is often described as a seaweedy, medicinal taste and a distinct peaty flavour.

Lowland malts are drier when compared to their Highland counterparts, and although often quite spirity, are light whiskies which generally have fewer individual differences than the whiskies from other regions.

Northern Highland malts are sweeter and have more body and character than their Lowland relations. They can have very distinctive and subtle characters, with a rich mellowness and fullness of flavour, but, equally, they can show a dry peatiness or a delicate fragrance.

The Speyside malts are the sweetest whiskies. And, although they do not have as much body as other Highland malts, their flavours are richer and more complex, with fruity, leafy and honeyed notes and a subtle delicacy of aroma which, once recognised, should be easy to identify.

Eastern Highland malts come from the area between Aberdeen and Speyside. Often full bodied, they tend to have a dry, fruity-sweet flavour, together with a touch of smokiness.

The Perthshire malts, although Highland by definition, come from the area bordering the Lowland region. They tend to be dry, clean tasting whiskies which are both light and fruity. Their identity may best be considered as falling somewhere between that of Lowland and Speyside whiskies.

The Island malts from Skye, Jura, Mull and Orkney are characterised by a peaty, smoky nose and flavour. Some could be said to more closely resemble Islay malts while others are more like Northern Highland whiskies.

If it is possible to categorise Campbeltown nowadays, then it must fall between the Lowlands and the Highlands in dryness, but shows a distinct smoky character with good body.

Irish malt whiskey is much lighter, smoother and mellower than its Scottish counterparts. This is, in part, due to the fact that it is triple distilled, although there are two or three Scottish single malts also produced in this way.

Although it is possible to map out generalised characteristics for single malts, each distillery produces a malt which has its own unique personality. It has its own micro-climate, wild yeasts, source of water and specified malting requirement. All of these factors, and even the shape of the still used, will have an effect on the individual character and flavour of a malt.

John Lamond

John Lamond, who compiled the tasting notes, is an acknowledged expert on malt whisky. Born in Perth, he has worked in the Scottish licensed trade for most of his life. He is secretary of the Institute of Wines and Spirits (Scotland) and in 1987 he won the prestigious Tamnavulin Master of Malt Competition. John is a director of The Malt Whisky Association.

File notes

The notes in this book have been compiled in alphabetical order of available brands of whisky, not by distillery or bottler. Where the whisky is only available from an independent source, this has been noted in the text.

Remember that the malts covered in this book are single malts — the product of one named distillery only. The blending of these whiskies may only be carried out with other malts from the same source if the term "single malt" is to be used on the bottle.

"Vatted malts", on the other hand, are whiskies from more than one malt distillery which have been blended together according to the specifications of the blender, to produce a fine, consistent product which may well be given an individual name (such as *Strathconon*). Vatted malts have not been included in the tasting notes.

Certain companies and groups are mentioned throughout the text in abbreviated form. The following are the principal ones:

IDV   International Distillers and Vintners
SMD   Scottish Malt Distillers (now United Malt and Grain Distillers Limited)
IDG   Irish Distillers Group
ABD   Arthur Bell Distillers (A division of Guinness plc)
DCL   The Distillers Company Limited

Gordon & MacPhail
> An independent bottler, from whom certain of the malts mentioned in the notes are available. Based in Elgin.

Wm Cadenhead
> Similarly an independent bottler mentioned throughout the notes. Based in Campbeltown, but the company also has a shop in Edinburgh.

Hints on pronunciation

Unless you are an expert Gaelic speaker, you may have difficulty in pronouncing some of the names of the malts in this book, or the areas in which they are produced. The following list contains those that may cause a slight problem, with their phonetic alternatives in italics, thus:

Slainte	*Schlan-jer*
Auchentoshan	*Ochentoshan*
Auchroisk	*Othrusk*
Bruichladdich	*Brew-ich-laddie*
Bunnahabhain	*Boonahavun*
Caol Ila	*Kaaleela*
Cardhu	*Kar-doo*
Clynelish	*Klynleesh*
Craigellachie	*Krai-GELLachy*
Dailuaine	*Dall-yewan*
Dallas Dhu	*Dallas Doo*
Edradour	*Edra-dower*
Glen Garioch	*Glen Gear-ee*
Glenglassaugh	*Glen Glas-och*
Glen Mhor	*Glen Vor*
Glenmorangie	*Glen-MORanjee*
Glentauchers	*Glen-tockers*
Islay	*I-lay*
Knockdhu	*Nock-doo*
Laphroaig	*La-froyg*
Old Pulteney	*Pult-nay*
St Magdalene	*Magdaleen*
Strathisla	*Strath-eye-la*
Tamdhu	*Tam Doo*
Tamnavulin	*Tamnavoolin*
Teaninich	*Tea-aninich*
Tomintoul	*Tomintowel*
Tullibardine	*Tully Bard-eye-n*

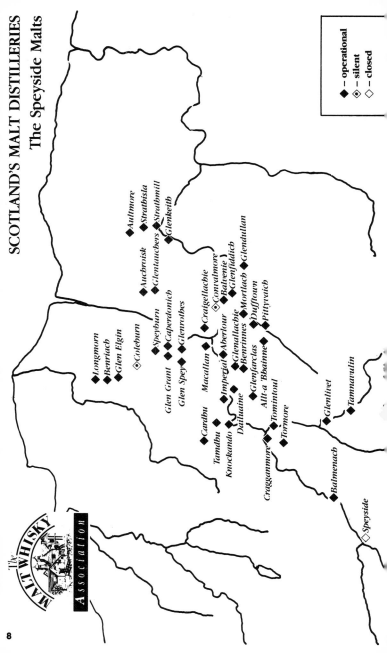

SCOTLAND'S MALT DISTILLERIES
The Speyside Malts

- operational
- silent
- closed

Aultmore
Strathisla
Strathmill
Auchroisk
Glentauchers
Glenkeith
Craigellachie
Convalmore
Balvenie
Glenfiddich
Glendullan
Speyburn
Caperdonich
Glenrothes
Colehurn
Longmorn
Benriach
Glen Elgin
Macallan
Imperial
Aberlour
Glenallachie
Benrinnes
Mortlach
Dufftown
Pittyvaich
Glen Grant
Glen Spey
Caradhu
Glenfarclas
Allt-a-'Bhainne
Glenlivet
Tammavulin
Tamdhu
Knockando
Dailuaine
Tomintoul
Tormore
Cragganmore
Balmenach
Speyside

The MALT WHISKY Association

8

The art of 'nosing'

It seems somewhat perverse that those who appreciate one of the finest drinks these islands have ever produced spend a great deal of their time not drinking it.

They do not even go so far as those serious-minded wine connoisseurs who swill it round their mouths before ejecting it.

No. The master blender will use nothing other than his nose — and his experience — to assess and evaluate malt whisky.

The reason for this is to preserve the ability to "taste" after the first sample. Because unlike wine or other less alcoholic substances, a distilled spirit will vitally affect those very taste mechanisms which need to be used again and again.

The experts have another explanation for using the nose rather than the mouth to detect flavour. They say it is more direct.

Our sense of aromatics (or "volatiles", as they are sometimes called), is derived from an area known as the olfactory epithelium, which has a direct link to the brain. It is located at the back of the nasal passage, and is one of the main reasons why we cannot "taste" so well when we have a cold.

Using the nose to detect the aromatic ingredients provides a more immediate route to this area than through the back of the throat. There is, of course, a slight difference in the result and the strength of individual flavours may vary, but in general the nose is capable of detecting exactly same indicators as the mouth.

Our sense of smell is one of the most under-used of the human senses, being relegated in most cases by sight and taste to a subordinate role and only called into use for rather crude analysis of what smells "good" and what smells "bad". In fact, it is one of the most subtle of the senses, capable of detecting even faint changes in style or balance, and having a large "vocabulary" of its own. /continued

The master blender has an "educated" nose and can detect more than 150 separate flavours or effects in a product such as whisky. Some of these will tell him that the product has been adversely affected in some way during production. Others will indicate the type or style of wood in which the whisky has matured. But for you, the malt whisky drinker, there are sufficient indicators to allow you to tell one type of single malt whisky from another.

In general, the nosing of malt whisky is carried out in a small, tulip shaped glass or sherry copita which will allow the aromatics to be released from the spirit yet retained in the glass.

The sample is always diluted with water, the amount depending on the alcoholic strength of the whisky which is being "nosed". As a general guide, malt whisky in the strength band 40 — 43 per cent alcohol by volume should be diluted with an equal volume of water, preferably Scottish spring water or clean tap water. Avoid any water with a high chlorine content or other flavour which would affect the sample.

Other, higher strength whiskies should be diluted with a higher quantity of water, to bring the sample to approximately the same strength. For example, a high strength whisky of above 60 per cent abv should be diluted with three times its volume of water for sampling.

There is a very good reason for this. The olfactory senses are adversely affected by the higher alcoholic content, even to the extent of feeling pain. The dilution removes the painful effect while allowing the aromas present in the spirit to be released.

This result is assisted by swirling the mixture round the glass for a few seconds prior to nosing. This will release the aromatics which are then retained within the glass for sampling.

The quantity used for sampling should be fairly small, to allow plenty of room for the aromatics to collect in the glass. There is quite enough spirit for an adequate assessment in a diluted single measure or 25ml of whisky and water.

You will find that different elements in the sample become dominant at different periods of the nosing.

You will also find that as you become more expert, you are able to detect a greater range of "smells" in the single glass. This is the fascination of single malts. From the basic simple ingredients comes an enormous variety of styles and tastes which you are now beginning to explore!

The difficulty with either tasting or nosing is in the descriptions used by individuals to describe the sensation or flavour. Some attempt has been made to categorise these, even to the extent of producing a "Flavour Wheel" with such evocative descriptions as "newly sharpened pencils" or "crushed green bracken".

Our own Master of Malt — John Lamond — has used many of these expressions in the tasting notes in this book. Do not be deterred, however, by some of the expressions which he employs, which should not be taken too literally. After some experimentation yourself, you will undoubtedly see — or smell — what he means.

But while a standardised approach to taste or smell is sensible in the commercial sector, the malt whisky drinker recognises that taste and preference are highly subjective. What you derive from your nosing of malt whiskies may not be exactly the same as your friends or colleagues. You can have just as much fun trying to describe the aromas as accurately as possible as you do from tasting the whiskies!

A note on the water

Although in many parts of the world water from the kitchen tap is safe to drink, it is far from ideal as an accompaniment to malt whisky.

In some areas, the water is naturally quite chalky or perhaps, as in parts of Scotland, rather peaty. In others, for reasons of public health, various additives are put into water supplies. The water authorities in Britain, for example, add a certain amount of chlorine to drinking water. /continued

Such chemically treated water is not recommended if you wish to bring out the nose of your single malt to its best advantage.

Water filters can be one answer, but the best choice is clear, pure spring water which has been bottled at source. Go for Scottish water if you wish, but there are also other quality choices available.

Choose a still water rather than a sparkling one, however, and avoid the more strongly flavoured waters. They may be excellent in their own right and their mineral content good for you, but they may adversely affect the delightful aroma of the malt.

Key to symbols

The following symbols are used at the head of each entry to denote the geographical area of production. For a comparison, see the article on pages 4 and 5.

H Highland

L Lowland

I Islay

S Speyside

C Campbeltown

IR Irish

Aberfeldy

Established	1896
Age/Strength	1970 distillation 40% abv
Distillery	Aberfeldy
Address	Aberfeldy, Perthshire
Map reference	NN 866495

Colour	Straw/golden with yellow highlights
Nose	Fresh, crisp, slightly peaty, surprisingly so for a malt from so far south
Finish	Reasonably long and clean
Flavour	Big, round, dry, slightly woody and malty
Water	Pitilie Burn
History	Built between 1896-8 by Perth-based blenders, John Dewar & Sons Ltd. Owned by Scottish Malt Distillers since 1930, having passed into the ownership of DCL in 1925. Now part of United Distillers plc.
Geography	Immediately to the east of the village on the main (now closed) railway line, main road and close to the river Tay.

Notes	Major rebuilding work took place in 1972, with four stills in a new stillhouse. Previously about a dozen distilleries had been opened in the Aberfeldy neighbourhood by men who had been smugglers in the mountains in earlier times. Gordon & MacPhail bottling.

Aberlour

Established	1826
Age/Strength	10 years 40% abv
Distillery	Aberlour
Address	Aberlour, Banffshire
Map reference	NJ 264424

Colour	Deep amber/golden
Nose	Full, rich, sweet, slightly toffee-like
Finish	Good full and long
Flavour	Fine, well balanced richness
Water	A spring on Ben Rinnes
History	Founded in 1826 by James Gordon and Peter Weir. Rebuilt in 1898 after a fire. Re-equipped with four stills in 1973. The Aberlour Glenlivet Distillery Co is a subsidiary of Campbell Distillers (itself part of Pernod Ricard).
Geography	Aberlour is situated about a quarter of a mile below the Lynn of Ruthrie, a 30 foot cascade on Ben Rinnes which falls into the pool which gives rise to the Burn called the Lour. The distillery is about 300 yards from the Lour's confluence with the River Spey.
Notes	Aberlour is a delightful village by the Lour at the foot of Ben Rinnes, from the summit of which ten counties, from Caithness to Perth, are visible. The early Christian missionary, St Dunstan (or St Drostan, as he was known in Scotland), used the waters of the Lour for baptisms. He became Archbishop of Canterbury in 960 AD.

Allt-a' Bhainne

Established	1975
Age/Strength	Not available in bottle
Distillery	Allt-a' Bhainne
Address	Near Dufftown, Banffshire
Map reference	NJ 264424

Colour	
Nose	
Finish	
Flavour	
Water	Springs on Ben Rinnes
History	A modern building, of modern architecture, built in 1975 by Chivas Brothers Ltd, a subsidiary of The Seagram Company of Canada. As a reminder of the traditional distillery, four small pagoda roofs are set on the main roof.
Geography	Sited on the southern slopes of Ben Rinnes to the north of the B9009 some 8 miles south west of Dufftown.
Notes	Allt-a' Bhainne is the Gaelic for "burn of milk". Its make is not available in bottle yet, but now that the earliest of the make is more than 12 years old, it is probably finding its way into Chivas Regal.

Ardbeg

Established	1794
Age/Strength	10 years 40%abv
Distillery	Ardbeg
Address	Port Ellen, Islay, Argyll
Map reference	NR 414462

Colour	Pale straw with golden reflections
Nose	Peaty with an unusual sweet edge
Finish	Long and smokey
Flavour	Full, peaty, rich with no hint of the sweetness indicated by the nose
Water	Supply from Lochs Arinambeast and Uigidale
History	The original distillery was run by a somewhat notorious band of smugglers, before Excise men overran the place, destroying the buildings. John McDougall established the present distillery in 1815. Owned by Hiram Walker, itself now part of Allied Lyons, since 1979.
Geography	A very romantic, lonely site at the water's edge on the south east coast of Islay.

Notes	The distillery is now closed but there is talk of it re-opening.

Ardmore

Established	1898
Age/Strength	15 years 45.7% abv
Distillery	Ardmore
Address	Kennethmont, Aberdeenshire
Map reference	NJ 553292

Colour	Very dark with rich deep amber highlights
Nose	Full, rich, medium-sweet with a distinctive syrupy peatiness
Finish	Spicy, vegetal greenness and dry, quite rich though
Flavour	Full, rich, sweet, complex flavours develop in the mouth — dry treacle, leafiness, burnt heather
Water	Spring on Knockandy Hill
History	Built by Wm Teacher with two stills and doubled in size twice — four stills in 1955 and eight stills in 1974. The distillery was built as part of a major expansion programme for the company's popular blended whiskies.
Geography	Situated alongside the Aberdeen to Inverness railway, below the 1,425 ft Knockandy Hill. Close by is Leith Hall.

Notes	Bottled by Wm Teacher. Limited supplies available. Wm Teacher use the make in blending "Highland Cream".

Ardmore

Age/Strength	18 years 46% abv

Colour	Full amber with golden highlights
Nose	Light, slightly sweet and oaky
Finish	Very fine, creamy and oaky
Flavour	Malty, richly sweet and full

Notes	Wm Cadenhead bottling.

Auchentoshan

Established	c 1800
Age/Strength	10 years 40% abv
Distillery	Auchentoshan
Address	Dalmuir, Dunbartonshire
Map reference	NS 478726

Colour	Very pale straw, slight green edge
Nose	Fresh, clean, floral aroma
Finish	Quite good but light
Flavour	Light, soft, sweet and slightly fruity
Water	Near Cochna Loch in the Kilpatrick Hills
History	The name Auchentoshan is believed to be derived from the Gaelic words "achadh oisinn" possibly meaning "corner of the field". Not much is known of the distillery's early years, but a Mr Thorne has been recorded as owning it in 1825. It is now one of three distilleries owned by Morrison Bowmore Distillers. Although not the only distillery to experience war damage, (see Banff) it had the misfortune to suffer heavily from enemy bombing, an event which caused extensive damage and a great loss of spirit!
Geography	The distillery is situated next to the Erskine Bridge overlooking the River Clyde.

Notes   Although geographically situated south of the Highland line, the source of Auchentoshan's water supply is north of the line. Thus the distillery is a Lowland one but its water supply is Highland. The make is triple distilled and very lightly peated. The first distillation takes an hour, the second five and the third nine hours.

Aultmore

Established	1895
Age/Strength	12 years 40% abv
Distillery	Aultmore
Address	Keith, Banffshire
Map reference	NJ 401534

Colour	Pale golden
Nose	Fresh, lightly peated and slightly sweet
Finish	Light and warming
Flavour	Medium-bodied, slightly fruity
Water	The burn of Auchinderran
History	Built by Alexander Edward of Sanquhar Forres with two stills. The first of the make was produced in early 1897. Became part of DCL in 1925 and transferred to SMD in 1930. Rebuilt in 1970/1 and doubled to four stills. Now part of United Distillers plc.
Geography	An isolated building standing on the A96 Keith to Elgin road close to the turning to Buckie.

Notes	Until 1969 a steam engine had been providing power, operating 24 hours a day, seven days a week since 1898. The old engine is still kept for show.

Balblair

Established	1790
Age/Strength	5 years 40% abv
Distillery	Balblair
Address	Edderton, Ross-shire
Map reference	NH 706855

Colour	Very pale straw
Nose	Peaty, aromatic, quite light and spirity
Finish	Shortish and light
Flavour	Slightly sweet, faintly peaty, spirity and quite light
Water	The Ault Dreag, a burn four miles from the distillery
History	The present distillery was built in 1872, when the then owner, Andrew Ross, decided to extend the business, the new buildings being higher up the slope of the hill. The older buildings were converted into a bonded warehouse. Extended from two to three stills in the 1970s by owners, Hiram Walker, now part of Allied Lyons. The fermenting of ale on the site is said to have taken place as long ago as 1749.
Geography	Less than a quarter of a mile from the Dornoch Firth, about six miles from Tain on the A9.

Notes	Distilling in the area predates Balblair by more than a century, there being many suitable sources of water, and peat in abundance. Indeed, the Edderton area is known as the "parish of peats" and once abounded in smuggling bothies. One of the malts associated with Ballantine's blended Scotch whisky.

Balmenach

Established	1824
Age/Strength	1970 distillation. 40% abv
Distillery	Balmenach
Address	Cromdale, Morayshire
Map reference	NJ 078271

Colour	Straw/golden
Nose	Light but faintly sweet
Finish	Full and distinguished
Flavour	Much bigger than the nose suggests, a little woody and with a pleasant sweet edge
Water	The Cromdale Burn
History	The distillery was established in 1824 by James McGregor. At the time it was at the centre of an area which was full of smugglers' bothies, and illicit distilling was a way of life. Bought by SMD in 1930 and extended from four to six stills in 1962. Now part of United Distillers plc.
Geography	The distillery lies in a bowl in the hills off the A95 main road heading towards Bridge of Avon from Grantown-on-Spey.

Notes	The distillery stands about a mile from the former Cromdale station on the Spey Valley line. A branch was built to the distillery in the late 1880s and the steam engine which worked the line is preserved on the Strathspey railway at Aviemore. Gordon & MacPhail bottling.

The Balvenie (Founder's Reserve)

Established	1892
Age/Strength	10 years. 40% abv
Distillery	Balvenie
Address	Dufftown, Banffshire
Map reference	NJ 324414

Colour	Straw with good golden highlights
Nose	Full, rich with a green edge, medium-sweet, apples
Finish	Reasonable length, quite rich
Flavour	Medium-dry, smooth, oaky, malty
Water	The Robbie Dubh (pronounced "doo") spring
History	Built next to William Grant's Glenfiddich distillery in 1892. The stills came second-hand from Lagavulin and Glen Albyn. Three further stills were added to make eight in all (two in 1965 and one in 1971).
Geography	Situated just below Glenfiddich on the lower slopes of the Convals, the hills which dominate Dufftown.

Notes	The Balvenie is an excellent example of just how different single malts can be. Standing next door to its more famous sister, Glenfiddich, it draws its water from the same source and shares the same supply of malt — and yet the two whiskies are very different in character.

Banff

Established	1863
Age/Strength	1974 distillation 40% abv
Distillery	Banff
Address	Banff, Banffshire
Map reference	NJ 668643

Colour	Medium-peaty gold
Nose	Quite peaty, slightly oily with a hint of ozone
Finish	Good, long, slightly sugary-sweet, a little overpoweringly so
Flavour	Sweet, round, mellow, slightly spicy
Water	Springs on Fiskaidly Farm
History	Built by James Simpson junior, to replace an earlier distillery of the name built in 1824. Rebuilt after a fire in 1877. Owned by SMD since 1932. Two stills.
Geography	Half a mile west of Banff on the B9139

Notes	One of the earliest distilleries to be located in order to take advantage of the railways, although Banff's rail connection has long since been axed. On Saturday, 16 August 1941 a single German plane machine-gunned and bombed No. 12 warehouse. Exploding whisky casks flew through the air, and the local paper said, "Thousands of gallons of whisky were lost, either burning or running to waste over the land ... even farm animals grazing in the neighbourhood became visibly intoxicated." It is said that cows were not milked because they could not be got on their feet. Now closed. Gordon & MacPhail bottling.

Ben Nevis

Established	1825
Age/Strength	22 years 46% abv
Distillery	Ben Nevis
Address	Lochy Bridge, Fort William
Map reference	NN 126757

Colour	Deep peaty amber with good gold highlights
Nose	Spirity, malty, dryish, lightly peated, slightly leafy
Finish	Smooth, clean and enjoyably long
Flavour	Dry, lightly peaty, spirity, slightly spicy
Water	Buchan's Well on Ben Nevis
History	Founded by "Long John" Macdonald in 1825. Owned by various Macdonalds until bought by Seager Evans Ltd in the 1920s. Taken over by Ben Nevis Distillery (Fort William) Ltd, who installed a Coffey still. Four pot stills. Sold by the Whitbread group to the Japanese company, Nikka, early in 1989.
Geography	Is situated two miles north of Fort William on the A82.

Notes	A cask of Ben Nevis was presented to Queen Victoria on her visit to Fort William in 1848. The cask was not to be opened until the Prince of Wales attained his majority 15 years later. Wm Cadenhead bottling.

Benriach

Established	1898
Age/strength	1969 distillation 40% abv
Distillery	Benriach
Address	Longmorn, near Elgin, Morayshire
Map reference	NJ 230585

Colour	Pale straw with gold highlights
Nose	Sweet, distinctive fruitiness, fresh appley
Finish	Spicy, good with the apple flavour lingering
Flavour	Sweet, appley, distinctive, reminiscent of Calvados
Water	Local springs
History	Founded in 1898 as the whisky market moved into recession. It was then closed in 1900 and did not re-open until 1965, when it was rebuilt by The Glenlivet Distillers Ltd. Owned by The Seagram Company of Canada since 1977. Four stills.
Geography	Situated three miles south of Elgin to the east of the A941.

Notes	The floor maltings are still in use. Gordon & MacPhail bottling.

Benrinnes

Established	1835
Age/strength	1968 distillation 40% abv
Distillery	Benrinnes
Address	Aberlour, Banffshire
Map reference	NJ 259397

Colour	Straw/gold with good bright highlights
Nose	Sweet, nutty, slightly fatty
Finish	Good, smokey and dry, smooth and creamy
Flavour	Medium-sweet, smokey, spicy, oaky
Water	The Scurran and Rowantree Burns
History	The original distillery was located at Whitehouse Farm, three quarters of a mile to the south east, and was washed away in the great flood of 1829. The present distillery was founded in 1835 by William Smith & Co as an extension of the farmsteading. Acquired by Dewar's in 1922, becoming part of the DCL in 1925. Run by SMD since 1930. Doubled from three to six stills in 1966. Major reconstruction took place between 1955 and 1956. Now part of United Distillers plc.
Geography	Situated on a loop of an unclassified road, one and a half miles south of the A95, between it and the B9009.

Notes	After 1956 the distillery was more easily run, more productive but less picturesque. Visitors leaving the office no longer encountered cows (and a bull) emerging from the byres. There had even been times when employees had to abandon distilling to round up cattle. A form of triple distillation is practised. Gordon & MacPhail bottling.

Benromach

Established	1898
Age/Strength	1968 distillation 40% abv
Distillery	Benromach
Address	Forres, Morayshire
Map reference	NJ 033593

Colour	Deepish amber, slight grey-green tints
Nose	Full, ripe, sweet and definitely fruity
Finish	Spicy, long, perhaps a little floral
Flavour	Sweet, mellow, soft, a little spirity
Water	Chapeltown springs near Forres
History	Built by the Benromach Distillery Company. Bought by the DCL in 1953 and transferred to SMD. Now part of United Distillers plc. Rebuilt in 1966 and again in 1974. Two stills.
Geography	Sited to the north of Forres on the north side of the railway.

Notes	In 1925 the mash tun was wooden. Benromach has high pitched gables and narrow mullioned windows in the Scots vernacular style of the 17th century. Closed. Gordon & MacPhail bottling.

Ben Wyvis

Established	1965
Age/Strength	No sample available
Distillery	Ben Wyvis
Address	Invergordon, Ross & Cromarty
Map reference	NH 713690

Colour	
Nose	
Finish	
Flavour	
Water	Castle Dobbie reservoir
History	Built by the Invergordon Distillers Ltd, it completed its last distillation in 1976.
Geography	Invergordon is just off the A9 to the north of Inverness. It looks across the Cromarty Firth to the Black Isle.

Notes	Ben Wyvis was two pot stills situated within the Invergordon grain distillery complex.

Bladnoch

Established	1817
Age/strength	8 years 40% abv
Distillery	Bladnoch
Address	Bladnoch, Wigtown
Map reference	NX 421543

Colour	Light amber
Nose	Very light, dry
Finish	Slightly spirity, but lasts well
Flavour	Light, delicate and dry
Water	The river Bladnoch
History	Founded in 1817 by John and Thomas McClelland. Closed in 1938 and re-opened in 1956. Extended from two to four stills in 1966. Now part of United Distillers plc.
Geography	The southernmost distillery in Scotland. Situated on the river of the same name just a mile outside Wigtown.

Notes	Close to the distillery is Baldoon Farm, where stands the ruined castle to which Janet Dalrymple, the "Bride of Lammermoor" came to die after her marriage to David Dunbar of Baldoon,

Blair Athol

Established	1798
Age/Strength	8 years. 40% abv
Distillery	Blair Athol
Address	Pitlochry, Perthshire
Map reference	NN 946577

Colour	Straw/golden
Nose	Fresh, clean and lightly peated
Finish	Quite good and distinctive
Flavour	Sweet, almost almondy
Water	From a spring on the nearby 2,760 ft Ben Vrachie.
History	Although originally founded almost 30 years earlier, the present distillery was established in 1826 when revived by John Robertson. It passed into the hands of Alexander Conacher and Co in 1827. It closed in 1932, and although purchased the following year by Arthur Bell and Sons, did not come to life again until 1949, when it was rebuilt. Extended from two to four stills in 1973. Now part of United Distillers plc.
Geography	Not at Blair Athol as its name suggests. It is to be found on the southern approach road to Pitlochry, just off the new A9.

Notes	The distillery now has a large new visitors' centre. The Conacher family, who owned the distillery for a time in the 1800s, are said to be descended from the chivalrous young Conacher who so admired Catherine Glover, the Fair Maid of Perth.

Bowmore

Established	1779
Age/Strength	12 years 40% abv
Distillery	Bowmore
Address	Bowmore, Islay
Map reference	NR 309599

Colour	Full, amber, very bright
Nose	Lightish, peaty, burnt heather, characteristic tang of ozone/iodine and even a whiff of chocolate
Finish	A good long dry finish
Flavour	Smooth, refined flavour with a pronounced peatiness
Water	Laggan River
History	In 1776, an Islay merchant, David Simpson, obtained permission from the local laird to build dwellings and "other buildings". The "other buildings" were soon converted into a distillery. Bought by Stanley P. Morrison in 1963. Now owned by Morrison Bowmore Distillers.
Geography	Bowmore stands, almost fortress-like, on the shores of Loch Indaal.

Notes	Uses a revolutionary waste heat recovery system to cut costs. The distillery was built early in the village's history at the foot of Hill Street, and has proved important to its economic survival. Said to be the oldest legal distillery on the island.

Braes of Glenlivet

Established	1973
Age/Strength	Not available in bottle
Distillery	Braes of Glenlivet
Address	Near Tomintoul, Banffshire
Map reference	NT 243205

Colour	
Nose	
Finish	
Flavour	
Water	Two local wells — the Preenie and Kates's Well
History	Built by Chivas Bros Ltd, a subsidiary of The Seagram Company of Canada. Originally just three stills, but two more were added in 1975 and a sixth in 1978.
Geography	Situated near Chapeltown off the B9008 Tomintoul to Bridge of Avon road.

Notes	An attractive modern building, built in 1973 with pagodas incorporated into the roofline despite the fact that it does not have a floor maltings.

Brora

Established	1819
Age/Strength	Not bottled as Brora (see notes below)
Distillery	Brora
Address	Brora, Sutherland
Map reference	NC 897053

Colour	Clynemilton Burn
Nose	Originally called Clynelish, the distillery was founded
Finish	by the Marquis of Stafford, later the first Duke of
Flavour	Sutherland. It was intended as a ready market for
Water	barley produced by crofters who had been evicted
History	from inland farms and moved down to the coastal
	plain. Established as a brewery in 1817, it was turned
	into a distillery two years later. Operated by SMD
	since 1930. Two stills. It was renamed Brora in 1969
	after the new Clynelish distillery opened next door.
	Now part of United Distillers plc.
Geography	Just off the A9 at Brora. Brora distillery is sited on the
	north side of the extensive plain which forms the
	mouth of Strath Brora.

Notes

Brora was known as Clynelish until 1969. After the modern distillery had been built in 1967-68, the old "Clynelish" re-opened in April 1975, housed in the rebuilt old Brora mash house. It subsequently ceased distillation in May 1983. Some of the make can be obtained from independent bottlers, but there is confusion as it is often called Clynelish which, of course, it was. But it was never bottled as Brora, only as Clynelish prior to 1967. Between 1967 and 1983 output was stencilled as "Brora" on cask heads, although it has only been sold as "Clynelish" for fillings.

Bruichladdich

Established	1881
Age/Strength	10 years 40% abv
Distillery	Bruichladdich
Address	Bruichladdich, Islay
Map reference	NR 264612

Colour	Pale golden with slight green tinges
Nose	A delicate peatiness, fairly light with no great pungency
Finish	Good length with a well defined finish
Flavour	Full and flavoursome, smokey and dry, without the heavy notes of other Islays
Water	A reservoir in the local hills
History	Built by Robert, William and John Gourlay Harvey (of the Dundashill and Yoker Harveys). Became the Bruichladdich Distillery Co (Islay) Ltd in 1886. Doubled from two to four stills in 1975. Now owned by Invergordon Distillers.
Geography	Sited on the western side of the island, about two miles from Port Charlotte, on the opposite side of Loch Indaal to Bowmore.

Notes	The distillery is the most westerly in Scotland. A handsome building, built in a square; entry is through an archway. Its westerly position is thought to have a bearing on the lighter flavour it has compared with other Islay malts. Islay itself was the medieval seat of the Lords of the Isles.

Bruichladdich

Age/Strength	15 years 40% abv

Colour	Straw with amber-gold highlights
Nose	Rich, delicately peated, with underlying sweetness
Finish	Spicy, warm, long with sweet oak, but finally dry
Flavour	Sweet with hints of nuttiness, uncharacteristic of an Islay malt

Bunnahabhain

Established	1880
Age/Strength	12 years 40% abv
Distillery	Bunnahabhain
Address	Near Port Askaig, Islay
Map reference	NR 420732

Colour	Straw with golden highlights
Nose	Distinctive and flowery
Finish	Lovely, round and long
Flavour	Smoother, softer and less pungent than other Islays
Water	River Margadale
History	Became part of Highland Distilleries in 1887 when amalgamated with W. Grant and Co of Glenrothes. Extended from two to four stills in 1963.
Geography	Situated towards the north east tip of Islay on the bay from which it takes its name.

Notes	Bunnahabhain means "mouth of the river". Prior to the building of this distillery, which is Islay's most northerly, the adjacent area was inhospitable and uninhabited. Now a small hamlet has built up around the distillery.

Bushmills Malt

Established	1608
Age/Strength	10 years 40% abv
Distillery	Bushmills
Address	Bushmills, Co. Antrim, Northern Ireland
Map reference	East 9437 North 4052

Colour	Deep amber with gold reflections
Nose	Lightly peated, slightly oily, grassy
Finish	Long, fine and almost vinous or grapey
Flavour	Delicately sweet, quite complex, round, mellow, slightly spicy
Water	Saint Columb's Rill
History	Bushmills was granted a licence to distil in 1608, making it by the far the earliest legal distillery of all. Operated by Irish Distillers, in 1988 the target of a hard fought takeover battle between the British giant Grand Metropolitan and French rival Pernod Ricard which the latter won.
Geography	Situated on the north coast of Ulster, close to the Giant's Causeway.

Notes	Bushmills is triple distilled, a fact which is widely advertised, although it is not alone in this respect. The Scottish malts Auchentoshan, Benrinnes and Rosebank are also triple distilled. Bushmills Malt is also available in duty-free markets at 43% abv.

Caol Ila

Established	1846
Age/Strength	12 years 63% abv
Distillery	Caol Ila
Address	Port Askaig, Islay
Map reference	NR 433695

Colour	Amber-peaty with good gold highlights
Nose	Peaty, burnt heather, quite earthy, medicinal
Finish	Smooth, smokey, spicy, very long
Flavour	Medium-sweet, rich smokey, spicy, full, burnt heather
Water	Loch Nam Ban (Torrabolls Loch)
History	Built by Hector Henderson. Extended and rebuilt by Bulloch, Lade & Co in 1879. Came under the control of the DCL in 1927 and transferred to SMD three years later. The premises were completely rebuilt, apart from the warehouses, between April 1972 and January 1974 when extended from two to six stills.
Geography	Almost literally at the end of the road — the northern end of the A846.

Notes	"Caol Ila" is the Gaelic name for the Sound of Islay, the strait that separates Islay from Jura. Hot water from the distillery is pumped through sea water condensers, cooled and returned for re-use. Bottled by James MacArthur & Co. The richness derives from the sherry casks used for ageing.

Caol Ila

Age/Strength	1972 distillation 40% abv (Gordon & MacPhail bottling)

Colour	Palish gold with green tinges
Nose	Peaty, almost medicinal, strange touch of sweetness
Finish	Long, distinguished and smokey
Flavour	Heavy, clean, peaty, burnt heather with more than a tang of ozone.

Caperdonich

Established	1897
Age/Strength	1979 distillation. 40% abv
Distillery	Caperdonich
Address	Rothes, Morayshire
Map reference	NJ 278496

Colour	Pale straw. Almost yellow
Nose	Sweet, ripe, grapey with a hint of cloves
Finish	Quite good for its youth, but shortish
Flavour	Sweet, slight flavour of cloves, spirity
Water	The Caperdonich Well, adjacent to the Glen Grant Burn.
History	Following the industry slump at the turn of the century, Caperdonich was closed in 1902 and did not produce again until 1965, following rebuilding. Extended from two to four stills in 1967. Now owned by The Seagram Company of Canada.
Geography	Situated across the road from its sister, Glen Grant.

Notes	The distillery was built to supplement the output of Glen Grant and was known as Glen Grant No. 2. The whisky, using the same water, is lighter and fruitier than Glen Grant. The two distilleries were originally joined by a pipe which carried spirit from Caperdonich to Glen Grant across the town's main street. Gordon & MacPhail bottling.

Cardhu

Established	1824
Age/Strength	12 years 40% abv
Distillery	Cardhu
Address	Knockando, Morayshire
Map reference	NJ 191431

Colour	Straw/gold
Nose	Full, slightly peaty and sweet
Finish	Long, peaty and sweet
Flavour	Round, mellow and sweet; delicate peatiness
Water	Springs on the Mannoch Hill or the Lyne Burn
History	Built on a farm known as Cardow, and called until recently by that name. Acquired by John Walker and Son in 1893, becoming part of DCL in 1925. Transferred to SMD in 1930. Rebuilt in 1960 and extended from four to six stills. Now part of United Distillers plc.
Geography	Situated high up above the River Spey on its north side, on the B9102 between Knockando and Craigellachie.

Notes	The "flagship" of the United Distillers Group, the malt has long played an important role in Johnnie Walker's famous Red and Black Label brands. Cardhu means black rock. A very large reception centre was opened in 1988.

Clynelish

Established	1967
Age/Strength	12 years 40% abv
Distillery	Clynelish
Address	Brora, Sutherland
Map reference	NC 897053

Colour	Pale straw with lovely golden edges
Nose	Dry with a touch of sweetness on the edge. Slightly fruity and softly peaty
Finish	Long, dry and smokey
Flavour	Full bodied, slightly creamy and spicy
Water	Clynemilton Burn
History	Now part of United Distillers plc. Six stills.
Geography	Just off the A9 at Brora. Clynelish distillery is sited on the north side of the extensive plain which forms the mouth of Strath Brora.

Notes	Built next door to the old "Clynelish" distillery. A new visitors' centre opened in 1988.

Coleburn

Established	1897
Age/Strength	1965 distillation 40% abv
Distillery	Coleburn
Address	Longmorn, Elgin, Morayshire
Map reference	NJ 240553

Colour	Warm peaty/gold with amber highlights
Nose	Sweet, nutty, almondy, oily rich
Finish	Smooth, good length
Flavour	Medium-sweet, delicate, slightly spirity, rich
Water	A spring in the Glen of Rothes
History	Built by John Robertson & Son. Became part of DCL in 1925 and transferred to SMD in 1930. Two stills.
Geography	Situated to the east of the A491, four miles south of Elgin. It is "faced on one side by a ... plantation of Scotch firs and birches, and swept by the cool mountain breezes of Brown Muir" according to Robertson's original announcement in 1896.

Notes	The distillery was built in warm-coloured Morayshire sandstone and roofed with blue Welsh slates. A problem which faced the architect was the provision of a lavatory to the Excise Office — it took 18 months to resolve! The Excise Officer's house took even longer to be completed. Closed. Gordon & MacPhail bottling.

Convalmore

Established	1893
Age/Strength	1969 distillation 40% abv
Distillery	Convalmore
Address	Dufftown, Banffshire
Map reference	NJ 322418

Colour	Very pale straw, almost watery
Nose	Sweet, with the smell of a cornfield after rain in summer
Finish	Spicy, reasonable length
Flavour	Medium-sweet, nutty, spicy
Water	Springs in the Conval Hills
History	Founded 2 June 1893 by the Convalmore-Glenlivet Distillery Co Ltd. Fire broke out on 29 October 1909 and the malt barn, kiln, malt mill, mash house and tun room were destroyed. At its height the flames rose to between 30 and 40 feet. Snow also began to fall, providing a never to be forgotten spectacle. Rebuilt after the fire, experiments then being made with the continuous distillation of malt. Passed to DCL in 1925 and transferred to SMD in 1930. Doubled to four stills in 1964.
Geography	Situated three quarters of a mile north of Dufftown on the A941.

Notes	The distillery accommodated a signals detachment of the 51st (Highland) Division from 1940 to 1942 and then gunners of the 52nd (Lowland) Division until 1944. Closed. Gordon & MacPhail bottling.

Cragganmore

Established	1869
Age/Strength	12 years 40% abv
Distillery	Cragganmore
Address	Ballindalloch, Banffshire
Map reference	NJ 064264

Colour	Straw/gold
Nose	Quite dry for a Speyside, nonetheless a richness is present
Finish	Long and distinguished, slightly smokey
Flavour	Round, malty, medium-sweet and classy
Water	Craggan Burn — a spring on the Craggan More Hill
History	Built by John Smith, formerly the lessee of Glenfarclas. Rebuilt 1902. Extended from two to four stills in 1964.
Geography	Cragganmore occupies a site north of the A95 between Grantown-on-Spey and Ballindalloch, very close to the River Spey itself.

Notes	Originally only available at the distillery or through independent bottlers, the make is now more readily available. An interesting feature is that the spirit stills have T-shaped lye pipes instead of the usual swan necks. Each arm of the T has its own condenser. One of the United Distillers Classic Malts portfolio.

Craigellachie

Established	1891
Age/Strength	15 years 46% abv
Distillery	Craigellachie
Address	Craigellachie, Banffshire
Map reference	NJ 285452

Colour	Very pale, almost crystal clear watery coloured
Nose	Pungent, peaty, burnt heather, slight orangey edge
Finish	Good, spicy, long, reminiscent of Islay
Flavour	Heavy, pungent, peaty, an edge of sweetness
Water	A spring on the hill of Little Conval
History	Built by the Craigellachie Distillery Co Ltd, a partnership formed by a group of blenders and merchants. Acquired by the DCL in 1927 and transferred to SMD in 1930. Rebuilt in 1964-65 and doubled to four stills. Now part of United Distillers plc.
Geography	The distillery stands on the spur of a hill, the precipitous Rock of Craigellachie, overlooking the village of Craigellachie from the south.

Notes	Sir Peter Mackie, founder of White Horse, was one of the original owners. The workers in 1923 lived in tied cottages and tended their gardens carefully. The owners of the best kept gardens received prizes annually from the directors. Wm Cadenhead bottling.

Dailuaine

Established	1852
Age/Strength	23 years 46% abv
Distillery	Dailuaine
Address	Carron, by Aberlour, Banffshire
Map reference	NJ 237410

Colour	Very pale straw, slightly green tinge
Nose	Slightly medicinal, sweet, slightly smokey
Finish	Fine, smooth, nice sweetness
Flavour	Very sweet, peppery, fruity, spicy
Water	The Bailliemullich Burn
History	Said to have been built by a Mr Mackenzie, was amalgamated with Talisker on Skye and Imperial in 1898 to form Dailuaine-Talisker Distilleries Co Ltd. Became part of DCL in 1925 and run by SMD. Rebuilt after a fire in 1917 and again in 1959-60 when increased from four to six stills. Now part of United Distillers plc.
Geography	Situated on an unclassified road between the A95 and the B9102 at Archiestown. It is to the south of the River Spey.

Notes	"Dailuaine" is the Gaelic word meaning "green vale". It is situated in a hollow by the Carron Burn. Although electricity reached the Carron area in 1938, it was not introduced to Dailuaine until 1950. For some years from the late 1880s the distillery operated a rail link to the Spey Valley line at Carron station, a few hundred yards away. The steam locomotive which once worked the line is preserved on the Strathspey Railway. Wm Cadenhead bottling.

Dallas Dhu

Established	1899
Age/Strength	1969 distillation 40% abv
Distillery	Dallas Dhu
Address	Forres, Morayshire
Map reference	NJ 036567

Colour	Peaty/gold, good yellow highlights
Nose	Sweet, oaky, malty
Finish	Woody, dry, good vanilla finish
Flavour	Medium-sweet, peppery, good body
Water	The Altyre Burn (known locally as the Scourie Burn)
History	Originally to be called Dallasmore in 1898, the fillings were advertised as Dallas Dhu in November 1899 when it came on stream. Bought by DCL in 1929 and handed over to SMD to operate the following year. The stillhouse was burned down on 9 April 1939. It did not re-open until 1947, but has recently closed for good.
Geography	Built in a hollow to the east of an unclassified road which forks south of the A940 on the southern outskirts of Forres. The distillery is approximately one mile down this road.

Notes	The distillery buildings have been handed over by Scottish Malt Distillers to the Historic Buildings and Monuments department of the Scottish Office who are presenting them as a model example of a distillery on the tourist trail. It is still possible to obtain special bottlings from old casks. Gordon & MacPhail bottling.

Dalmore

Established	1839
Age/Strength	12 years 40% abv
Distillery	Dalmore
Address	Alness, Ross-shire
Map reference	NH 666687

Colour	Full deep amber with good gold highlights.
Nose	Slightly sweet, light oak, almost fruity
Finish	Lightly malty, smooth, quite distinguished
Flavour	Full, sweet, quite round, spicy, slightly smokey
Water	The River Alness, which flows from Loch of Gildermory, close to Ben Wyvis.
History	Much of the distillery was burnt down during US naval use during World War I. Production resumed in 1922. Doubled from four to eight stills in 1966. Two of the stills in use today date from 1874.
Geography	Situated just off the A9, the distillery is in a beautiful position overlooking the Black Isle across Cromarty Firth.

Notes	The distillery was well situated by its founders in the middle of a fine barley growing district. In the First World War, the distillery was used by the US Navy as a base for manufacturing deep sea mines. Bottled by Whyte & Mackay.

Dalwhinnie

Established	1897
Age/Strength	15 years 43% abv
Distillery	Dalwhinnie
Address	Dalwhinnie, Inverness-shire
Map reference	NN 638854

Colour	Straw/golden, honey-like
Nose	Aromatic with a light peatiness
Finish	Good, slightly sweet richness
Flavour	Round, with a honey-like richness
Water	Lochan an Doire-Vaine
History	Originally called Strathspey, its name was changed to Dalwhinnie when it was sold to Cook and Bernheimer of New York for #1,250 in 1905. Sold to Macdonald Greenlees of Edinburgh in 1919. Acquired by DCL in 1926 and then transferred to SMD. Badly damaged by fire in 1934, re-opening in 1938. Now part of United Distillers plc.
Geography	The distillery is situated at the junction of the A9 (Inverness to the north, Perth to the south) and the A889 to Fort William.

Notes	"Dalwhinnie" derives from the Gaelic word meaning "meeting place". Built in 1897 for close to £10,000, Dalwhinnie distillery is station 0582 of the Met. Office. The distillery is the focal point of the local community. At 1,100 feet above sea level, Dalwhinnie is Scotland's highest distillery. This is a new introduction, one of the United Distillers' Classic Malts portfolio.

Dalwhinnie

Age/Strength	8 years 40% abv

Colour	Lightish straw/golden
Nose	Light, spirity, aromatic
Finish	Quite good, spirity
Flavour	Lightish but round, medium-sweet.

Deanston

Established	1965
Age/Strength	8 years 40% abv
Distillery	Deanston
Address	Doune, Perthshire
Map reference	NN 715017

Colour	Pale straw/yellowish
Nose	Sweet, oily, almost fatty
Finish	Quite good and smooth
Flavour	An almost fruity sweetness, unusual for a malt from so far south
Water	River Teith
History	Founded by the Deanston Distillery Co Ltd and sold to Invergordon in 1972. Four stills. The original mill, designed by Richard Arkwright of "Spinning Jenny" fame, forms part of an extended complex of buildings.
Geography	Situated on the south bank of the river Teith within two miles of the centre of Doune village.

Notes	Was originally a textile mill dating from 1784, both ventures requiring good water supplies. The River Teith, as well as supplying all the process water, once drove a generator providing the distillery with electrical power.

Dufftown

Established	1887
Age/Strength	10 years 40% abv
Distillery	Dufftown
Address	Dufftown, Banffshire
Map reference	NJ 323389

Colour	Straw/golden
Nose	Light, burnt rubber, floweriness in background
Finish	Lasts well, but rubberiness stays with it
Flavour	Medium-sweet, slightly fruity, smooth
Water	Jock's Well, rising in the Conval Hills
History	Converted from a former meal mill. Purchased by Arthur Bell and Sons in 1933. Originally with two stills, extended to four in 1974 and six in 1979. Now part of United Distillers plc.
Geography	Situated in the Dullan Glen on the outskirts of Dufftown near the 6th century Mortlach parish church.

Notes	From Dufftown which has always been a source of good whisky. Rome was built on seven hills, Dufftown was built on seven stills.

The Edradour

Established	1825
Age/Strength	10 years 40% abv
Distillery	Edradour
Address	Moulin, Pitlochry, Perthshire
Map reference	NN 959579

Colour	Richly golden, gloriously viscous
Nose	Sweet, almondy aroma with a slight fruitiness
Finish	A buttery aftertaste
Flavour	A smooth, malty taste with a hint of dryness
Water	A spring on Ben Vrackie
History	Founded on land rented from the Duke of Athol, Edradour appears little changed by the passing of time. The distillery has gone through several interesting changes of ownership, the most notable of which was becoming a subsidiary of William Whitely and Co, which it was for most of the 20th century. It is now owned by Campbell Distillers, a subsidiary of the French company, Pernod Ricard, who are investing substantially behind both the development of the distillery and its single malt.
Geography	Situated at the roadside at the foot of a steep hill; a collection of ancient farmstead-like buildings, past which tumbles a quick flowing stream.

Notes	Scotland's smallest distillery whose actual output is only 600 gallons (3,600 bottles) per week. The last remaining of the once numerous Perthshire "farm" distilleries, and the last actually distilling by hand. It is run by just three people. The output of the single malt is 2,000 cases a year, the balance being kept as 'top dressing' principally for the "House of Lords" blend. Also known previously as Glenforres, which name is also now given to a vatting of several single malts, of which The Edradour is one.

Glen Albyn

Established	1846
Age/Strength	1963 distillation 40% abv
Distillery	Glen Albyn
Address	Inverness
Map reference	NH 654459

Colour	Peaty/gold with greenish tinges
Nose	Sweetish, creamy, fruity, hints of almond
Finish	Fine, long and delicately sweet
Flavour	Sweet, nutty, creamy
Water	Loch Ness
History	Founded by the then Provost of Inverness, James Sutherland. Rebuilt 1884 after being used as a flour mill following a period of disuse. Acquired by the DCL in 1972 and transferred to SMD. It had two stills, but is now silent for good.
Geography	Sited on the east side of the A9 on the north side of Inverness, it faced Glen Mhor distillery across the Great North Road where it crosses the Caledonian Canal.

Notes	The distillery was closed between 1917 and 1919 and used as a U.S. naval base for the manufacture of mines. For a long time supplies were delivered by sea. Demolished in 1988, along with Glen Mhor, to make way for a supermarket development. Prior to 1745, Inverness had been the chief malting town in Scotland. A story about Glen Albyn relates that a pipe was once laid from the distillery's spirit safe to a public house nearby. The pipelayer was transported to Australia for another matter, but when he returned some years later he informed the excise men. The pub lost its licence as a result and its customers perhaps rather more. Gordon & MacPhail bottling.

THE MALT FILE

Glenallachie

Established	1968
Age/Strength	12 years 40% abv
Distillery	Glenallachie
Address	Ruthie, Aberlour, Banffshire
Map reference	NJ 264412

Colour	Pale, soft golden
Nose	Full and delightfully leafy
Finish	Elegant
Flavour	Full-bodied and slightly sweet
Water	Springs near Ben Rinnes
History	Closed in 1987, when sold by Scottish and Newcastle to the Invergordon Distillers. Four stills.
Geography	The distillery nestles at the foot of Ben Rinnes, a short way from the A95.

Notes	A whisky of quality and greatly under-rated. The distillery is now mothballed, but has great promise for the future. One of three distilleries designed by Delme Evans, the other two being Jura and Tullibardine. As this book went to press, the distillery was acquired by the French Pernod Ricard group, which also owns Aberlour, Edradour and Bushmills (q.v.).

Glenburgie

Established	1829
Age/Strength	1960 distillation 40% abv
Distillery	Glenburgie
Address	Alves, near Forres, Morayshire
Map reference	NJ 097602

Colour	Pale straw, good yellow highlights
Nose	Woody, sweetish, slightly floral
Finish	Oaky, reasonable length
Flavour	Medium-sweet, slightly spicy, oaky, quite heavy
Water	Local springs
History	Founded on this site as Kinflat by William Paul, the grandfather of a celebrated London surgeon of the latter part of the 19th century, Dr Liston Paul. Silent 1927-35, and acquired by Hiram Walker in 1930. Now part of Allied Lyons. Two stills.
Geography	Sited in a valley to the south of the A95 some five miles east of Forres

Notes	The distillery did once have two short-necked "Lomond" stills which produced a heavier malt. One of the main malts associated with Ballantine's blended Scotch whisky. Gordon & MacPhail bottling.

Glencadam

Established	1825
Age/Strength	21 years 46% abv
Distillery	Glencadam
Address	Brechin, Angus
Map reference	NO 601608

Colour	Straw/gold, slight greenish tinges
Nose	Sweet, oily, slight sugar icing nose
Finish	Quite good but with a strange cold aftertaste
Flavour	Medium-sweet, spirity, smooth
Water	Springs in the Unthank Hills
History	Said to have been founded in 1825, the distillery passed through a number of owners until purchased by Hiram Walker & Sons (Scotland) Ltd in 1954. Now part of Allied Lyons, and operated by Stewart & Son of Dundee Ltd. Two stills.
Geography	Situated half a mile to the east of the town of Brechin in the cleft of a hill. Also about half a mile from the River Esk.

Notes	Presently only available through independent bottlers, in this case Wm Cadenhead. Some of the make goes into Stewart's Cream of the Barley blended Scotch whisky.

Glen Deveron

Established	1962
Age/Strength	12 years 40% abv
Distillery	Macduff
Address	Banff, Banffshire
Map reference	NJ 694633

Colour	Pale straw with bright golden highlights
Nose	Fresh, leafy, quite full
Finish	Lasts very well, distinguished
Flavour	Medium-sweet, very smooth
Water	The Gelly Burn
History	Acquired by William Lawson in 1972, who in turn became part of the General Beverage Corporation, the Luxembourg company which controls Martini and Rossi's world interests, in 1980. Extended from two to three stills in 1966 and to four in 1968.
Geography	Situated to the east of Banff on the east bank of the River Deveron, about half a mile from the Moray Firth.

Notes	The malt takes its name from the close-by River Deveron, rather than the distillery itself. It can also be obtained as special bottlings as Macduff.

Glendronach (Sherry Cask)

Established	1826
Age/Strength	12 years 40% abv
Distillery	Glendronach
Address	Forgue, near Huntly, Aberdeenshire
Map reference	NJ 624440

Colour	Quite dark and richly demerara
Nose	Rich, full, sweet with a smokey edge
Finish	Long with hints of shortbready sweetness in the aftertaste
Flavour	Rich, full with a slight maltiness
Water	"The Source" — a spring to the east of the distillery about four miles distant
History	One of the earliest licensed distilleries in Scotland. Its founder, James Allardes, was a frequent guest of the 5th Duke of Gordon, who was largely repsonsible for the Act of Parliament in 1823 which provided for the licensing of distilleries and reduced taxation — thus helping to bring about an end to the days of illicit distilling and whisky smuggling. Purchased by Wm Teacher and Sons Ltd in 1960.
Geography	Situated straddling the Dronach Burn, which supplies the cooling water, in the valley of Forgue. The distillery is set among tall trees in which rooks nestablished These are said to bring luck.

Notes	Aged in sherry casks. Also available as "Original". Built in the form of a square and covering four acres, Glendronach is one of the few distilleries where barley is malted on the premises. Traditional practice plays an important role in The Glendronach's processes. For example, floor maltings, coal fired stills and earth floored warehouses. Local barley is also used, coming from the company's own estates which surround the distillery.

Glendronach (the Original)

Age/Strength	12 years 40% abv

Colour	Straw with gold highlights
Nose	Slightly sweet, biscuity, quite mellow and buttery.
Finish	Slightly spicy, biscuity, good length
Flavour	Medium-sweet, soft, mellow, round.

Notes	Glendronach Original is aged in a combination of plain oak and sherry oak casks.

Glendullan

S

Established	1897
Age/Strength	12 years 43% abv
Distillery	Glendullan
Address	Dufftown, Banffshire
Map reference	NJ 329404

Colour	Pale golden with a slightly greenish edge
Nose	Full, fruity with a distinctly sweet oaky nose
Finish	Long and lingering, sweet and memorable
Flavour	Full, round, warm, sweet and spicy, slight flavour of coffee and toffee
Water	Springs in the Conval Hills
History	The last distillery to be built at Dufftown just before the turn of the century. Two stills. Rebuilt 1962. A modern distillery addition with six stills was built alongside in 1972. Now part of United Distillers plc.
Geography	Close by the junction of the A941 and A920.

Notes	Process water comes from the River Fiddich.

Glen Elgin

Established	1898
Age/Strength	12 years 43% abv
Distillery	Glen Elgin
Address	Longmorn, Elgin, Morayshire
Map reference	NJ 237573

Colour	Pale gold with peaty depths
Nose	Sweet, slightly green with fine, soft oak and hints of honey
Finish	Smooth and distinguished
Flavour	Soft, pleasantly sweet, smooth, round with honey coming through on the palate
Water	Springs near Millbuies Loch
History	Built in 1898-1900 by a partnership of William Simpson and James Carle. Acquired by SMD in 1930. Extended from two to six stills when rebuilt in 1964. Now part of United Distillers plc.
Geography	Situated on the main Elgin to Rothes road.

Notes	A very compact distillery due to shortage of capital when it was built. Sixty years were to elapse between the building of Glen Elgin and the next Highland distillery, Tormore distillery on Speyside. An important constituent of the White Horse blend, as witnessed by the white horse on the Glen Elgin label.

Glenesk

Established	1897
Age/Strength	12 years 40% abv
Distillery	Glenesk
Address	Hillside, by Montrose, Angus
Map reference	NO 718615

Colour	Pale straw/yellowish gold
Nose	Spirity, light with a hint of sweetness
Finish	Dry, reasonable length with a malty end to it
Flavour	Quite sweet, full, but with an almost unpleasant spiritiness
Water	The river North Esk
History	Closed during the First World War and not re-opened until 1938, when it was re-equipped to produce grain whisky as Montrose Distillery. Acquired by DCL in 1954 and operated off and on until 1964 when it was transferred to SMD who converted it again to a malt distillery. Renamed Glenesk in 1980.
Geography	Two miles north of Montrose, half a mile west off the A92, south of the river North Esk.

Notes	Established in 1897 on a former flax spinning mill site. Has been called Highland Esk, North Esk, Montrose, Hillside, and finally Glenesk. The distillery is now closed again, but the maltings are in full production for United Distillers Group.

Glenfarclas 105

Established	1836
Age/Strength	Minimum 8 years (bottled at 60% abv cask strength — 105‰ proof)
Distillery	Glenfarclas
Address	Ballindalloch, Banffshire
Map reference	NJ 212383

Colour	Deep peaty amber with gold highlights
Nose	Very spirity, slightly astringent, slightly sweet
Finish	Long, flavoursome, quite dry
Flavour	Spirity, malty, a little oily, slightly astringent
Water	Springs on Ben Rinnes
History	Founded by Robert Hay, a tenant farmer. Acquired by John Grant, who let it to John Smith from 1865-70. Run by the Grant family ever since. Extended from two to four stills in 1960 and to six in 1976.
Geography	South of the A95 almost midway between Grantown-on-Spey and Craigellachie, lying in desolate moorland at the foot of Ben Rinnes.

Notes	Reports indicate that the make ages very well. "Whisky Tom" Dewar waxed most eloquent of a 30-year old he tasted in 1912, although George Grant considers the 15-year old to be perfection — all a matter of personal taste. Glenfarclas is available at a number of different ages. Excellent reception centre. As the emphasis of Glenfarclas 105 is on its cask strength, there is now no age statement on the label. Youngest bottlings are of eight-year old, with the most recent being almost ten years old.

Glenfarclas

Age/Strength	10 years 40% abv

Colour	Straw with good gold highlights
Nose	Sweet leafy oak, slight tang of coffee
Finish	Slightly spicy, long and characterful
Flavour	Sweet, smooth, quite rich, malty

Glenfarclas

Age/Strength	15 years 46% abv

Colour	Peaty-amber with rich golden highlights
Nose	Full, quite rich, delicately peated
Finish	Smooth, smokey and quite long
Flavour	Medium-sweet, oaky, hints of burnt peat

Glenfarclas

Age/Strength	21 years 43% abv

Colour	Quite dark amber with rich gold highlights
Nose	Full, rich, sweet, slightly minty, also oak
Finish	Lightly smokey, rich and long lasting
Flavour	Rich, big, full-bodied, slightly smokey

Glenfiddich

Established	1887
Age/Strength	8 years 40% abv
Distillery	Glenfiddich
Address	Dufftown, Banffshire
Map reference	NJ 323411

Colour	Straw/gold
Nose	Cooked mash, light, soapy, delicately peaty
Finish	Sweet, medium length
Flavour	Light, sweet, well balanced and gentle
Water	The Robbie Dubh spring
History	When Alfred Barnard published his Whisky Distilleries of Scotland in 1887, the home of the best selling single malt in the world had only just been built. Owned by William Grant and Sons Ltd it today boasts 28 stills, 10 wash and 18 spirit. No mean achievement for a distillery founded with £120 capital and using equipment from the old Cardow distillery; but such has been the success of the family enterprise founded by William Grant of Glenfiddich — the son of a soldier who had served under Wellington.
Geography	Situated on the outskirts of Dufftown

Notes	One of only three malt whiskies bottled at the distillery, the others being Lochside and Springbank. The first distillery in Scotland to open a reception centre, it now attracts well over 100,000 visitors a year. The distillery welcomed its one millionth visitor, Ronald Pedersen, with his wife Peggy, in August 1987.

Glenfiddich

Age/strength	**18 years 43% abv**

Colour	Straw with greeny gold highlights
Nose	Rich, medium-sweet, grapey, quite soft, slight hint of coffee
Finish	Good, smooth, long with hints of coffee
Flavour	Medium-sweet, spicy, slightly peppery, slight green-leafiness

Glen Flagler

Established	1965
Age/Strength	Sample not available
Distillery	Moffat
Address	Moffat, by Airdrie, Lanarkshire
Map reference	NS 790647

Colour
Nose
Finish
Flavour
Water
History   Built by Inver House Distillers Ltd. Converted in 1965 from Moffat Mills paper mill to a plant producing grain whisky and neutral spirit. Within the complex were pot stills producing malt whisky marketed as "Glen Flagler".

Geography

Notes   Moffat was originally known as Garnheath. Now demolished.

Glen Garioch

Established	1797
Age/Strength	10 years 40% abv
Distillery	Glen Garioch
Address	Old Meldrum, Aberdeenshire
Map reference	NJ 808276

Colour	Bright gold
Nose	Delicately peaty and smokey, flowery
Finish	Good, smooth, delicate
Flavour	Peaty, reminiscent of Islay, dry and slightly pungent
Water	Springs on Percock Hill
History	Established by one Thomas Simpson. In almost two centuries, ownership has passed through various hands, including SMD who acquired it in 1943. It was closed by them in 1968 and sold to Stanley P. Morrison who extended it from two to three stills in 1973. Now owned by Morrison Bowmore Distillers.
Geography	The distillery is situated in Old Meldrum village, close by the historic Meldrum House.

Notes	Garioch is pronounced "Geerie". Waste heat and COEX are used to grow tomatoes. The malt has only recently been made generally available in bottle. The Garioch valley, an 18 mile or so stretch of highly fertile land is known as the granary of Aberdeenshire. Glen Garioch was indeed a canny place to site a distillery.

Glenglassaugh

Established	1875
Age/Strength	Sample not available
Distillery	Glenglassaugh
Address	Near Portsoy, Banffshire
Map reference	NJ 562659

Colour	
Nose	
Finish	
Flavour	
Water	The Glassaugh Spring
History	Founded by the Glenglassaugh Distillery Co, Glenglassaugh was silent from 1907 to 1931 and from 1936 until it was extensively rebuilt by Highland Distillers in 1959. Two stills.
Geography	Sited in the Glassaugh Glen to the north of the A98 approximately two miles west of Portsoy, on the slope of a steep hill near to the sea.

Notes	Very rarely available as a single. The distillery was considered to be very advanced for its day when built.

Glengoyne

Established	1833
Age/Strength	10 years 40% abv
Distillery	Glengoyne
Address	Old Killearn, Dumgoyne, Stirlingshire
Map reference	NS 527686

Colour	Very pale gold
Nose	Light, fresh, floral
Finish	Reasonable length with a creamy tail
Flavour	Dry with a touch of sweetness, peppery and smooth
Water	A burn which falls down Dumgoyne Hill, known locally as the Distillery Burn.
History	Originally known as Burnfoot. Owned by Lang Brothers since 1876, the company becoming part of the Robertson & Baxter group in 1965. Rebuilt in 1966-7 and extended from two to three stills.
Geography	At the foot of Dumgoyne Hill, at the north west end of the Campsie Hills, with a new visitor centre overlooking a 50 foot high waterfall. The distillery is sited on the Highland line, but as its waters come from the north of it, it is classified as a Highland malt.

Notes	Although first licensed in 1833, the distillery is believed to be somewhat older. Was triple distilled in Victorian times but now only double distilled. The make is reduced using natural spring water. Not far from the distillery is the hollow tree in which Rob Roy MacGregor, immortalised by Sir Walter Scott, is reputed to have hidden while fleeing from law enforcement officers.

Glengoyne

Age/Strength	17 years 43% abv

Colour	Pale peaty with yellowy-golden highlights
Nose	Rich, sweet, oak, light fruit and toffee, almost liquorice
Finish	Spicy, malty and of nice length, quite chewy
Flavour	Soft, rich, smooth, with sweet oaky vanilla

Glen Grant

Established	1840
Age/Strength	No age statement 40% abv
Distillery	Glen Grant
Address	Rothes, Morayshire
Map reference	NJ 276495

Colour	Light gold/copper
Nose	Light, somewhat hard and astringent
Finish	Reasonable length with a strange heathery tang
Flavour	Drier than most Speyside malts, spirity, slightly peppery
Water	Glen Grant Burn
History	Founded by the brothers James and John Grant who had previously been distillers at nearby Aberlour. Amalgamated with George and J.G. Smith of The Glenlivet in 1953. Owned by The Seagram Company of Canada since 1977. Extended from four to six stills in 1973 and to eight in 1977.
Geography	At the northern end of the A941 as it passes through Rothes.

Notes	All but two of the Glen Grant stills are coal-fired, something of a curiosity nowadays. The other two are now heated by steam from a waste heat boiler, thus affording considerable energy conservation. It is not generally recognised that Glen Grant is the world's second best selling single malt, owing to its dominant position in Italy, where as a 5 year old it has around 70% of the considerable single malt whisky market. It is also Italy's best selling whisky. A supply of overproof Glen Grant is kept in a whisky safe built into the rock in the burn above the distillery. It is reached through an apple orchard. Taste it with water from the stream if you get the chance.

Glen Grant

Age/Strength   12 years

Colour   Straw/gold with amber highlights
Nose   Light, sweet, slightly fruity, still astringent
Finish   Dry, slightly astringent, lingering
Flavour   Light, medium-sweet, spirity, creamy

Notes   Available from independent bottlers.

Glen Grant

Age/Strength   15 years

Colour   Peaty/gold with good highlights
Nose   Sweet, lightish, nutty, slight fruitiness
Finish   The smokiness comes through on the finish which is smooth and mellow
Flavour   Medium-sweet, nutty, smooth, slightly smokey

Notes   Gordon & MacPhail bottling.

GlenKeith

Established	1957
Age/Strength	
Distillery	Glenkeith
Address	Keith, Banffshire
Map reference	NJ 427512

Colour	
Nose	
Finish	
Flavour	
Water	The Balloch Hill springs
History	Part of an original oatmeal mill of unknown age, it was converted to a distillery by Chivas Brothers Ltd, a subsidiary of The Seagram Company of Canada, between 1957 and 1960. Originally designed for triple distillation but converted to double distillation in 1970.
Geography	By the Linn pool near the centre of Keith.

Notes	It was the first distillery in Scotland to have a gas-fired still, and the first to use a microprocessor to control the whole operation.

Glenkinchie

Established	1837
Age/Strength	10 years 43% abv
Distillery	Glenkinchie
Address	Pencaitland, East Lothian
Map reference	NT 443668

Colour	Pale straw/golden with yellow highlights
Nose	Dry, pleasantly peated, slightly spirity
Finish	Long, lingering, delicately smokey and quite rich
Flavour	Dry, malty, quite spicy, full, smooth
Water	Reservoirs on the Lammermuir Hills
History	The distillery has long been involved in things agricultural, managers in past years having won fatstock prizes at Smithfield and Edinburgh, the beasts flourishing on the distillery by-products. Owned by SMD since 1914 and now licensed to John Haig & Co. Part of United Distillers plc.
Geography	Due south of Pencaitland, the distillery is in a hollow in the hills, and although the chimney can been seen for some distance, the road end can easily be missed as the sign is traditionally overgrown.

Notes	The distillery has a unique museum of distilling which includes an enormous scale model of a distillery. A new introduction, part of the United Distillers' Classic Malts portfolio.

Glenkinchie

Age/Strength	1974 distillation 40% abv

Colour	Light gold with bright highlights
Nose	Light, fresh and clean
Finish	Good, long, refined
Flavour	Dry with surprising depth and body for a Lowland

Notes	Gordon & MacPhail bottling

The Glenlivet

Established	1824
Age/Strength	12 years 40% abv
Distillery	The Glenlivet
Address	Minmore, Ballindalloch, Banffshire
Map reference	NJ 196290

Colour	Straw with a definite greenness to its edge
Nose	Leafy, floral, slightly malty and very fragrant
Finish	Good length
Flavour	Sherry cask comes through on the palate with the Glenlivet's typical honeyed sweet flavour
Water	Josie's Well
History	George Smith established his distillery in 1824 at Upper Drummin farm, being the first distiller in the Highlands to take out a licence after the passing of the Excise Act of 1823. After the original distillery had been destroyed by fire a new one was built at Minmore on land obtained from the Duke of Richmond. The very district of Glenlivet is rich in history. It was here that in 1594 the Royal army under the Earl of Huntly defeated the Covenanter forces commanded by the Duke of Argyle. The Glenlivet is now owned by The Seagram Company of Canada (see Glen Grant entry).
Geography	Situated on slopes of the Braes of Glenlivet, the local hills, it is in a relatively remote position, being four miles from the nearest village.

Notes	Though many others have laid claim to the Glenlivet appellation, there is only one distillery which can rightly be called "The Glenlivet", following legal action in the 1880s. So famous had Glenlivet already become by then that the wags of the day called it "the longest glen in Scotland".

Glenlochy

Established	1898
Age/Strength	1974 distillation 40% abv
Distillery	Glenlochy
Address	Fort William, Inverness-shire
Map reference	NN 113744

Colour	Palish amber, copper highlights
Nose	Spirity, sweet, woody, fruity
Finish	Short with a strange woody aftertaste
Flavour	Sweet, woody, creamy, spicy
Water	The River Nevis
History	Glenlochy has always been very up-to-date. Joseph Hobbs of Associated Scottish Distillers sold it in 1940. He established the Great Glen cattle ranch in 1948 which is still in operation. Silent 1919-24 and again 1926-37. Bought by DCL in 1953, when the operation was transferred to SMD. Two stills.
Geography[*]	Situated within Fort William on the north bank of the River Nevis to the north of the A82.

Notes	The old malt kiln has an exceptionally high pitched pagoda roof. Closed. Gordon & MacPhail bottling.

Glenlossie

Established	1876
Age/Strength	1968 distillation 40% abv
Distillery	Glenlossie
Address	Elgin, Morayshire
Map reference	NJ 213572

Colour	Palish gold with good bright highlights
Nose	Sweet, fruity, slightly musty, nutty
Finish	Nice fruitiness, good length, nutty on finish
Flavour	Sweet, fruity, musty, spicy
Water	The Bardon Burn
History	Built in 1876 by John Duff, tenant of the Fife Arms, Lhanbryde. Controlling interest obtained by SMD in 1919. Extended from four to six stills in 1962. The make is important to John Haig's blends, the distillery being licensed to the company. Now part of United Distillers plc.
Geography	Sited at Thornshill on an unclassified road to the west of the A941, two miles south of Elgin.

Notes	A purifier has been installed between the lyne arm and the condenser on each of the three spirit stills. Converted from steam power to electricity as late as 1960. Gordon & MacPhail bottling.

Glen Mhor

Established	1892
Age/Strength	8 years 57% abv
Distillery	Glen Mhor
Address	Inverness
Map reference	NH 654457

Colour	Straw/amber, good gold highlights
Nose	Lightly peated with an edge of sweetness
Finish	Spicy, creamy, long and almost leafy
Flavour	Medium-sweet, slightly woody, quite full
Water	Loch Ness
History	Founded by ex-provost John Birnie, Glen Mhor began production on 8 December 1894. It came into DCL in 1972, since when it was operated by Scottish Malt Distillers.
Geography	The distillery was situated at the north end of the Caledonian Canal where it intersects with the Great North Road (the A9) at the north west of Inverness. Across the road from Glen Albyn.

Notes	The name Glen Mhor means "Great Glen". The first distillery in Scotland to introduce mechanical malting, Glen Mhor, like Glen Albyn, is alas no more. Both were bulldozed flat in 1988 to make way for a supermarket. Gordon & MacPhail bottling.

Glenmorangie

Established	1843
Age/Strength	10 years 40% abv
Distillery	Glenmorangie
Address	Tain, Ross-shire
Map reference	NH 767838

Colour	Good light gold/pale straw
Nose	Slightly heavy, steely, fresh, hints of peat and floral note
Finish	Sweet with good length
Flavour	Light, slightly smokey, oily creaminess
Water	Springs in the Tarlogie hills above the distillery
History	Converted from the Morangie brewery of McKenzie and Gallie by William Matheson. Rebuilt in 1887 and again in 1979 when it was extended from two to four stills. Owned by Macdonald and Muir, the Leith blenders, since 1918.
Geography	Sited on the Dornoch Firth, on the A9 between Tain and Edderton, looking across the Firth towards the hills of Sutherland.

Notes	One of the smallest of all Highland distilleries. All of the make is used by the owners, none being made available as fillings. A noted feature of the distillery is that the stills have very tall necks, at 16′ 10″ (5.14 metres), the tallest in the Highlands. The water of the Tarlogie Spring is particularly hard and rich in mineral content taken from the red sandstone rock of the hills.

Glenmorangie

Age/Strength	25 year old (1963 distillation, bottled 1988) 43% abv

Colour	Quite pale peaty/straw with gold and green highlights
Nose	Rich, full malty, oaky with sweet appley fruit
Finish	Long, spicy, caramelly and fine
Flavour	Sweet, full spicy, quite green with a toffee-like richness

Glen Moray

Established	1897
Age/Strength	12 years 40% abv
Distillery	Glen Moray
Address	Elgin, Morayshire
Map reference	NJ 200624

Colour	Pale gold
Nose	Clean, fresh, aromatic, slightly peppery
Finish	Delicate, of reasonable length and soft
Flavour	Light, creamy, heathery, medium-sweet
Water	River Lossie
History	Like its sister distillery, Glenmorangie, a former brewery. Closed in 1910. Passed into the ownership of Macdonald and Muir in 1923. Rebuilt in 1979 when it was converted from two to four stills.
Geography	Situated in a hollow on the bank of the River Lossie, just outside Elgin.

Notes	Close by the distillery is Gallows Hill, as its name implies the scene of public hangings in days long gone. Some of the make goes into Macdonald and Muir's Highland Queen blended whisky.

Glenordie

Established	1838
Age/Strength	12 years 40% abv
Distillery	Ord
Address	Muir of Ord, Ross-shire
Map reference	NG 518508

Colour	Gold/straw, amber tints
Nose	Full, slightly dry but with an overlying richness
Finish	Very smooth, long and smokey
Flavour	Quite big, full, round, medium-sweet
Water	Loch Nan Eun and Loch Nam Bonnach
History	Founded as the Ord Distillery Co, under which name it traded until 1923 when it was sold to John Dewar and Sons of Perth. Incorporated in the DCL in 1925, and given to the control of SMD in 1930. Extended from two to six stills in 1966 when it was rebuilt. Now part of United Distillers plc.
Geography	To the west side of the A832 immediately to the west of Muir of Ord

Notes	The New Statistical Account of Scotland recorded in 1840 that "distilling of aquavitae" was the sole manufacture of the district. Ord — which is built on the site of a smuggler's bothy — is the only distillery remaining in the area.

Glenrothes

Established	1878
Age/Strength	16 years 46% abv
Distillery	Glenrothes
Address	Rothes, Morayshire
Map reference	NJ 272492

Colour	Deep gold, quite peaty in colour
Nose	Fruity, sweet, slightly oaky
Finish	Long, complex, dryish
Flavour	Full, richly sweet, possibly a little woody
Water	Springs in the hills above the distillery
History	Built by W. Grant and Co. Amalgamated with the Islay Distillery Co. to form The Highland Distilleries Ltd. Enlarged in 1963 from four to six stills and by a further two in 1980.
Geography	The distillery is situated a short way up the glen formed by the Burn of Rothes, which flows from the Mannoch Hills.

Notes	The first spirit ran from the stills on the night in 1897 of the Tay bridge rail disaster. The new stills are copies of the older ones. Wm Cadenhead bottling.

Glen Scotia

Established	1832
Age/Strength	8 years 40% abv
Distillery	Glen Scotia
Address	Campbeltown, Argyll
Map reference	NS 725210

Colour	Golden with hints of peaty water
Nose	Slightly peaty, complex but delicate
Finish	Soft and long
Flavour	Lightish, smokey, richly sweet, slightly spirity
Water	The Crosshill Loch and two wells bored 80 feet down into the rocks below the distillery
History	Said to have been founded by Stewart, Galbraith and Co. Various changes of ownership, the present owners being Gibson International Ltd. Two stills of classic swan necked design.
Geography	In the centre of the town at the intersection of High Street and Saddell Street.

Notes   One of only two distilleries remaining in Campbeltown (the other is Springbank q.v.) somewhat fewer than the 19 which existed at the start of the economic recession of the 1920s and early 30s, during which time all were closed. Glen Scotia and Springbank were the only two which re-opened. After £1 million had been spent upgrading the distillery between 1979 and 1982, it was then closed again. It re-opened in 1989.

Glen Spey

Established	c 1878
Age/Strength	8 years
Distillery	Glen Spey
Address	Rothes, Morayshire
Map reference	NJ 275492

Colour	Pale straw
Nose	Light, floral, spirity
Finish	Smooth and slightly sweet
Flavour	Strangely fragrant, almost perfumed, but velvety smooth
Water	The Doonie Burn
History	Established by James Stuart and Co. Owned by W. & A. Gilbey since 1887 and now ultimately owned by the Grand Metropolitan Group. Rebuilt in 1970 when it was extended from two to four stills.
Geography	The distillery stands just below the ruins of Castle Rothes, the ancient seat of the Leslie family, Earls of Rothes.

Notes	James Stuart and Co also once owned Macallan distillery, a short distance away at Craigellachie.

Glentauchers

Established	1898
Age/Strength	No sample available
Distillery	Glentauchers
Address	Mulben, Banffshire
Map reference	NJ 373498

Colour	
Nose	
Finish	
Flavour	
Water	Springs in the local hills
History	The foundation stone was laid on 29 May 1897. The original owner was James Buchanan, later Lord Woolavington of Black & White fame. This was his first venture into distilling. Became part of DCL in 1925, the distillery coming under the SMD operational wing in 1930. Rebuilt 1965-66 when increased from two to six stills.
Geography	On the A95, four miles west of Keith.

Notes	Experiments in the continuous distillation of malt whisky were carried out here around 1910.

The Glenturret

Established	1775
Age/Strength	8 years 40% abv
Distillery	Glenturret
Address	The Hosh, Crieff, Perthshire PH7 4HA
Map reference	NN 857233

Colour	Very pale straw with pale yellow-green highlights
Nose	Full, fruity, quite spirity, malty, dryish
Finish	Lightly spicy, grapey, medium length
Flavour	Light weight, medium-dry, round, smooth, slightly fruity
Water	Loch Turret
History	Glenturret, previously called Hosh, is the second to take that name. It was renamed Glenturret in 1875, some 20 or so years after the nearby original distillery of that name had closed. The distillery, which with two stills is one of the smallest in Scotland, was silent from 1923 to 1959.
Geography	Sited on the banks of the River Turret north west of Crieff on a secondary road which leads from the A85 round Crieff to Monzie and Gilmerton.
Notes	Glenturret is possibly Scotland's oldest distillery. Although the present buildings were erected in 1775, illicit distilling took place at least as early as 1717. The Drummond Arms Hotel at Crieff was the building in which Prince Charles Edward Stuart, Bonny Prince Charlie, held his stormy council of war on 3 February 1746. Apart from possibly being the oldest distillery in Scotland (see Littlemill q.v.). Glenturret has another impressive claim to fame in the Guinness Book of Records. A legend even in her lifetime, Towser, the distillery rodent operative, is credited with catching a world record total of 28,899 mice. Born at the distillery on 21 April 1963, Towser died on 20th March 1987, not far short of her 24th birthday. As well as the mice, Towser the cat was also more than a match for the rats, baby rabbits and even pheasants.

Glenturret

Age/Strength   10 years 57.1% abv

Colour	Very pale straw with pale yellowy-green highlights
Nose	Full, slightly sweet, floral, slightly malty
Finish	Smooth, dry, quite long with soft edges
Flavour	Quite full, round, smooth, creamy, slightly meaty, medium-dry

Age/Strength   12 years 40% abv

Colour	Straw/amber with good greeny-gold highlights
Nose	Rich, sherried, medium-sweet, oaky vanilla
Finish	Smooth, long, sherried
Flavour	Rich, medium-sweet, sweet oak, full, smooth

Age/strength   15 years 40% abv

Colour	Straw-amber with greeny-yellow highlights
Nose	Medium-sweet, rich, oaky-vanilla, liquorice, citrusy, minty
Finish	Smooth, spicy, good length and character
Flavour	Medium weight, quite rich, spicy, hints of mint and liquorice, very complex

Age/Strength   1972 distillation 40% abv

Colour	Pale straw with good greeny-gold highlights
Nose	Rich, vanilla, malty, medium-sweet, delicate oak
Finish	Smooth, pleasantly soft and reasonable length
Flavour	Rich, soft, round, hints of smokiness, medium-sweet

Glenugie

Established	1831
Age/Strength	No sample available
Distillery	Glenugie
Address	Peterhead, Aberdeenshire
Map reference	

Colour
Nose
Finish
Flavour

Water	Springs in the moors inland
History	Built by Donald, McLeod & Co. Unlike many distilleries which were originally breweries, Glenugie was converted into one for a while before being turned back to distilling. Became part of Long John International in 1970, which in turn was purchased by Whitbread in 1975. Two stills.
Geography	Sited some three miles south of Peterhead, Glenugie is positioned close to the sea, below the A92.

Notes	Closed in 1982. The distillery building, with its cast iron frames, is of unusual and interesting design.

Glenury-Royal

Established	1825
Age/Strength	12 years 40% abv
Distillery	Glenury-Royal
Address	Stonehaven, Kincardineshire
Map reference	NO 871868

Colour	Gold/copper
Nose	Light, spirity, malty, dry
Finish	Smokey but quite short
Flavour	Light, dry and slightly smokey
Water	Cowie Water
History	Originally built as a market for barley in a period of agricultural depression. It was taken over by an American firm, Associated Scottish Distillers, and was laid out as a model distillery in 1938. Purchased by the DCL in 1953 and transferred to SMD. Rebuilt in 1966 when it doubled in size to four stills.
Geography	On the north bank of Cowie Water on the northern outskirts of Stonehaven.

Notes	The water supply is also that of Stonehaven. The distillery is now closed with, it is believed, little hope of re-opening.

Highland Park

Established	1798
Age/Strength	12 years 40% abv
Distillery	Highland Park
Address	Kirkwall, Orkney
Map reference	HY 452095

Colour	Pale straw with pale yellow depths
Nose	Pleasantly peaty with a hint of smokiness
Finish	Long and distinguished
Flavour	Dry and well balanced
Water	From springs below the level of the distillery. The water has to be pumped uphill.
History	Founded by David Robertson. Enlarged from two to four stills in 1898 when owned by James Grant. Owned by Highland Distilleries since 1935.
Geography	Sited on a hillside, overlooking Scapa Flow to the south and Kirkwall to the north.

Notes	The distillery is built on the spot where the legendary 18th century smuggler Magnus Eunson's bothy stood. A local churchman as well as distiller, he apparently kept a stock of whisky under his pulpit. Hearing that his church was about to be searched by the excisemen, he had the kegs removed to his house where they were shrouded in white cloth. A coffin lid was placed next to the cloth and Eunson and his family knelt in prayer. The whispered word "smallpox" quickly ended any idea of a search by the excisemen. A visitors' centre was opened in 1987, a special feature of which is a 15 minute audio-visual presentation on the history and notable features of Orkney.

Imperial

Established	1897
Age/Strength	12 years 65% abv
Distillery	Imperial
Address	Carron, Morayshire
Map reference	NJ 222412

Colour	Slightly hazy, pale straw/yellow
Nose	Full, sweetish, malty, spirity
Finish	Long, quite spicy, strong and quite scented, strangely chocolatey
Flavour	Quite sweet, smooth, almost creamy, lightly smokey
Water	The Ballintomb Burn
History	Built by Thomas Mackenzie in 1897 and transferred to Dailuaine-Talisker Distilleries the following year. However, it was built at the time of the Pattisons blenders crash — a bad time for the industry and the beginning of a period of sharp contraction. Closed in 1899 and silent until 1919. Became part of the DCL in 1925, when it again closed. Re-opened under the control of SMD when rebuilt in 1955. Doubled to four stills in 1965.
Geography	Sited at a hollow on the banks of the Spey at Carron station on an unclassified road between the A95 and B9102, 1½ miles south west of Aberlour.

Notes	Bottled by James Macarthur & Co Ltd. The distillery is built of red Aberdeen bricks. One of the malt kilns was once surmounted by a large Imperial crown which flashed and glittered in the sunlight. The crown was taken down in 1955. Imperial was a billet for troops during the Second World War. To relieve the tedium, they threw hand grenades into the dam - it has leaked ever since. It was one of the distilleries where experimentation on effluent disposal as cattle feed was pioneered. Purchased by Allied Distillers in 1989.

Inchgower

Established	1871
Age/Strength	12 years 40% abv
Distillery	Inchgower
Address	Buckie, Banffshire
Map reference	NJ 427640

Colour	Pale golden/straw
Nose	Slightly sweet, peaty
Finish	Distinguished, long and delicately sweet
Flavour	Rich, sweet, full, with a delicate peatiness
Water	Springs in the Menduff Hills
History	Built by Alexander Wilson and Co to replace nearby Tochineal. Was owned by Buckie town council from 1936 to 1938 when it was sold to Arthur Bell and Sons for £1,000. Doubled to four stills in 1966. Now part of United Distillers plc.
Geography	Sited on the north side of the A98 between Fochabers and Buckie

Notes	A farm on the hill above the distillery was once the home of a noted local smuggler by the name of Macpherson. His still, well hidden at the back of the hill, was only discoverd when some stray Highland cattle dislodged a large piece of turf, thus exposing the still to the farmer driving the cattle home. Sad to say for Macpherson, the farmer was quick to tip off the excisemen and claim his reward.

Inchmurrin

Established	1965
Age/Strength	No age statement
Distillery	Loch Lomond
Address	Alexandria, Dunbartonshire
Map reference	NS 394806

Colour	Quite pale, good yellow highlights, slightly green
Nose	Malty, spirity, quite dry, slightly rubbery
Finish	The spirit follows through with an almost medicinal finish
Flavour	Spirity, quite dry but with a sweet edge, slightly spicy
Water	Loch Lomond
History	Built in 1965/6 by the Littlemill Distillery Co Ltd. Now owned by Glen Catrine Bonded Warehouse Ltd. Two stills.
Geography	Alexandria is at the southern end of Loch Lomond on the A82 Glasgow to Fort William road.

Notes	An earlier distillery of the same name existed at nearby Arrochar from about 1814 to 1817.

Inverleven

Established	1938
Age/Strength	Sample not available
Distillery	Inverleven
Address	Dumbarton, Dunbartonshire
Map reference	NS 398752

Colour	
Nose	
Finish	
Flavour	
Water	Loch Lomond
History	Built in 1938 by Hiram Walker & Sons, Scotland. Licensed to George Ballantine & Son Ltd. Now part of Allied Lyons.
Geography	

Notes	Two stills for producing malt whisky at the Dumbarton grain distillery complex. A third Lomond-type still is used to produce Lomond (q.v.)

Isle of Jura

Established	1810
Age/Strength	10 years
Distillery	Jura
Address	Isle of Jura, Argyll
Map reference	NR 526671

Colour	Pale straw with very slight green tinges
Nose	Full, pleasant, dry
Finish	Very delicate, lightly peated, very smooth and lingers well
Flavour	Very delicate, lightly peated, a pleasant oily/nuttiness
Water	Loch A'Bhaile Mhargaidh (Market Loch)
History	After passing through several different owners in its early years, Jura blossomed in the late 1800s after coming into the hands of Messrs James Ferguson and Sons in 1875, being rebuilt at a cost of £25,000. However, it closed in the early 1900s because, it is said, of an argument over the rent, after which the distiller upped and went, taking his still and equipment with him. It was abandoned until the late 1950s when a rebuilding programme was begun. The first spirit for more than 50 years flowed again in 1963. Enlarged from two to four stills in 1978. Now owned by Invergordon Distillers Ltd.
Geography	The island is situated north east of Islay. The distillery is on the leeward east coast of Jura, built on a bay where a string of islands forms a natural breakwater.

Notes	Records are said to trace illicit distilling on Jura as long ago as 1502. After the distillery had been rebuilt in the 1870s it gained a reputation for being one of the most efficient in Scotland. However, it was discovered that the spent wash from the stills was finding its way into a local cattle trough. The effect on the animals, it is said, was most interesting.

Kinclaith

Est	1957
Age/Strength	20 years 46% abv
Distillery	Kinclaith
Address	Moffat Street, Glasgow G5
Map reference	NS 598640

Colour	Very pale straw with yellow/green highlights
Nose	Sweet, oaky, rich, full
Finish	Peppery, spicy, dry
Flavour	Medium-sweet, creamy, smooth
Water	Local Glasgow water supply — Loch Katrine
History	Built 1957/8 within the Strathclyde Grain Distilling complex and dismantled in 1975 to make way for an enlarged Strathclyde.
Geography	

Notes	Wm Cadenhead bottling.

Knockando

Established	1898
Age/Strength	1974 distillation 40% abv
Distillery	Knockando
Address	Knockando, Morayshire
Map reference	NJ 195415

Colour	Honey-golden, quite pale
Nose	Lightish, sweet and leafy
Finish	Long, sweet, distinctive and fine
Flavour	Typical Speyside sweetness, full, round, good oak
Water	Cardnach spring
History	Built by Ian Thomson and acquired by W & A Gilbey in 1904. Now managed by Justerini & Brooks, a subsidiary of IDV Ltd, who are themselves part of the Grand Metropolitan Group.
Geography	South of the B9102 between Knockando and Archiestown, sited on the banks of the river Spey, close to Tamdhu distillery.

Notes	Much of the make is used in the J & B blend. An individual feature of the malt is that its bottle states both its year of distillation and date of bottling. If you believe that whisky, like wine, has vintage years then Knockando is worthy of a close study. Knockando is "Cnoc-an-Dhu" in Gaelic, which means "little black hillock".

Knockando
Extra Old Reserve

Age/Strength	21 years 43% abv

Colour	Straw, light peaty with pale greeny-gold highlights
Nose	Lightly peated, medium-dry, leafy, oaky, vanilla
Finish	Smooth, dryish, delicately spicy, quite long
Flavour	Medium-weight, slightly green, medium-dry, round

THE MALT FILE

Knockdhu

Established	1893/4
Age/Strength	1974 distillation 40% abv
Distillery	Knockdhu
Address	Knock, Banffshire
Map reference	NJ 547528

Colour	Pale straw/gold with yellow highlights
Nose	Fatty, slightly sweet, quite full
Finish	Quite long, slightly oily
Flavour	Sweet, malty, slightly peppery
Water	A spring on the southern slopes of Knock Hill
History	This was the first malt distillery to be owned by DCL. Sold in late 1988 to the Knockdhu Distillery Company Ltd. Two stills.
Geography	Sited to the west of the B9022, seven miles north of Huntly.

Notes	Built of fine local grey granite. The water supply, owned by the company, is supplied also to the villagers of Knock. It was occupied by a unit of the Indian Army from 1940 to 1945. The distillery was closed when purchased by its new owners but it re-opened in February 1989. Gordon & MacPhail bottling.

Ladyburn

Established	1966
Age/Strength	Sample not available
Distillery	Ladyburn
Address	Girvan, Ayrshire
Map reference	NX 200998

Colour
Nose
Finish
Flavour
Water
History   Opened in 1966 by William Grant & Sons Ltd, but
Ladyburn has not produced issue since 1976.
Geography   Ladyburn is part of the complex which includes the
Girvan grain distillery.

Notes   William Grant & Sons are also the proud owners of
the Speyside malts Glenfiddich and The Balvenie, but
Ladyburn is much harder to come by, as it is only
occasionally released through independent bottlers,
none being available from the owners.

Lagavulin

Established	1816
Age/Strength	12 years 40% abv
Distillery	Lagavulin
Address	Port Ellen, Islay
Map reference	NR 404457

Colour	Golden brown like a peat-stained burn
Nose	Big, powerful, burnt mahogany, lots of peat
Finish	Explosive, spicy and smokey
Flavour	Full, heavy, smokily powerful, strangely sweet edge
Water	Solan Lochs
History	Originally two distilleries were set up on the site, the first in 1816 and the second the following year. Lagavulin has long been important to the White Horse blended whisky, becoming part of the DCL in 1927. It was transferred to SMD in 1930. The distillery was rebuilt in 1962, when the stills from Malt Mill distillery were incorporated. Four stills. Now part of United Distillers plc.
Geography	Occupying a site of six acres, the distillery stands at the head of a small bay. The ruins of Dunyveg castle are at the entrance to the distillery.

Notes	Lagganmhouillin — or Lagavulin — means "Mill in the valley". Distilling on the site is thought to date from as early as 1742, when there were ten small bothies there.

Lagavulin

Age/Strength	16 years 43% abv

Colour	Amber with rich gold highlights
Nose	Distinctive, pungent, burnt heather, very peaty and full
Finish	Long, smokey, almost burnt, very lingering.
Flavour	Big, peaty, dry, very smooth and powerfully complex.

Laphroaig

Established	1820
Age/Strength	10 years 40% abv
Distillery	Laphroaig
Address	By Port Ellen, Islay
Map reference	NR 387452

Colour	Palish amber with slightly greenish tones
Nose	Dry, heavy, peaty and a heathery smokiness
Finish	Lingering and unique
Flavour	Full of character, very peaty, iodine/medicinal
Water	The Surnaig Burn
History	Said to have been founded by Donald and Alex Johnston. Now owned by James Burrough Distillers, part of Whitbread.
Geography	Situated in a small bay, frequented by otters and swans, it has been greatly influenced by the sea.

Notes Generally accepted as being the most individually flavoured of all single malts. Although Laphroaig, like all the distilleries on Islay, is built on the coast, it has always been maintained that it is not only the sea air but the peat which accounts for the distinctiveness of the make. The peat, it appears, is strongly impregnated with moss and this is said to give rise to Laphroaig's particular flavour. For 16 years, during the 1950s and 60s, Laphroaig had the distinction of being run by the only woman distiller in Scotland — one Miss Bessie Williamson.

Laphroaig

Age/Strength	15 years 40% abv

Colour	Amber/peaty with good gold highlights
Nose	Peaty, full, medicinal, slightly fruity edge
Finish	Long, smokey and refined
Flavour	Soft, smokey, round, smooth with a slightly sweet middle to the palate

Linkwood

Established	1821
Age/Strength	12 years 40% abv
Distillery	Linkwood
Address	Elgin, Morayshire
Map reference	NJ 233613

Colour	Clear golden, like sunlit peat-stained loch water over a sandy bottom
Nose	Fruity with a sweetness reminiscent of apples
Finish	Long and elegant
Flavour	Pleasantly light, round, sweet and slightly spicy
Water	Springs near Milbuies Loch
History	The original distillery was pulled down and rebuilt between 1872 and 1873. Became part of SMD in 1933. Rebuilt twice more in 1962 and 1971, when it was extended from two to six stills. Now part of United Distillers plc.
Geography	A very picturesque distillery with a reservoir of water, for cooling purposes, inhabited by swans, alongside the buildings.

Notes	Named after a former mansion house which once stood on the site. It is surrounded by woodland, hence its name.

Littlemill

Established	1772
Age/Strength	8 years 43% abv
Distillery	Littlemill
Address	Bowling, Dunbartonshire
Map reference	NS 442737

Colour	Pale straw with greeny-gold highlights
Nose	Full, fruity, medium-dry, malty, vanilla
Finish	Spicy, reasonable length and dry
Flavour	Soft, spicy, peppery, oatmealy, quite full
Water	A spring in the Kilpatrick Hills
History	The distillery has had numerous owners over its at least two centuries of operation, although its origins are somewhat obscure. Littlemill Distillery could be Scotland's oldest distillery. It is possible that whisky was distilled on the site as long ago as the fourteenth century, when the Colquhouns built Dunglass Castle to guard the ford across the Clyde. The distillery is now owned by Gibson International, a company formed following a management buy-out from previous owners The Argyll Group. Two stills.
Geography	Sited on the Clyde at the foot of the Kilpatrick Hills, 12 miles from Glasgow towards Dumbarton.

Notes	Although strictly speaking a Lowland malt, this is another which takes its water supply from north of the Highland line. Until the 1930s the make was triple distilled. The present stills are of a most unusual design.

Lochside

Established	1957
Age/Strength	No age statement 40% abv
Distillery	Lochside
Address	Montrose, Angus
Map reference	NO 715590

Colour	Light straw with gold highlights
Nose	Lightish, floral, leafy, slightly sweet
Finish	Leafy, hints of coffee, quite smooth
Flavour	Medium-dry, round, spicy, medium weight
Water	A bore well underneath the distillery
History	Converted from Deuchar's Brewery in 1957 by MacNab Distilleries Ltd as a malt and grain distillery, it was acquired by Distilerias y Crianza of Madrid in 1973. Originally four pot stills and one Coffey (grain) still, the latter being closed in 1970.
Geography	Lochside is at the north end of Montrose, on the coastal Aberdeen to Dundee road.

Notes	All of the make is bottled at the distillery by MacNab Distilleries. A small loch once existed opposite the distillery, hence the name Lochside. Most of the malt goes to export, with Spain being the major market, although it is also available locally.

Lomond

Established	1938
Age/Strength	Sample not available
Distillery	Inverleven
Address	Dumbarton, Dunbartonshire
Map reference	NS 398752

Colour	
Nose	
Finish	
Flavour	
Water	Loch Lomond
History	Built in 1938 by Hiram Walker & Sons, Scotland. Licensed to George Ballantine & Son Ltd. Now part of Allied Lyons.
Geography	

Notes	A Lomond-type still at Inverleven (q.v.) which is itself part of the Dumbarton grain distillery complex.

Longmorn

Established	1894
Age/Strength	15 years 43% abv
Distillery	Longmorn
Address	Longmorn, near Elgin, Morayshire
Map reference	NJ 234585

Colour	Straw, bright gold
Nose	Tremendously full, sweet and slightly peppery
Finish	Long, velvety, smooth and very elegant
Flavour	Full-bodied and buttery with a hint of nuttiness
Water	Local springs
History	Built by the Longmorn Distillery Co. Amalgamated with The Glenlivet and Glen Grant Distilleries and Hill, Thomson & Co Ltd to form The Glenlivet Distillers Ltd. Owned by The Seagram Company of Canada since 1977. Extended from four to six stills in 1972 and to eight in 1974.
Geography	On the A941 Elgin to Rothes and Craigellachie road.

Notes	Professor R.J.S. McDowall considered it to be one of the four finest malts. The name Longmorn comes from the Gaelic Lhanmorgund meaning "place of the holy man", the distillery reputedly being built on the site of an ancient chapel. The distillery houses an old steam engine which is occasionally used and also has a disused waterwheel. This malt is much favoured by blenders as a "top dressing" for their blends.

Longrow

Established	1973
Age/Strength	1973 distillation 43% abv
Distillery	Springbank
Address	Campbeltown
Map reference	NR 718205

Colour	Pale gold with green edges
Nose	Peaty, quite full with an edge of sweetness
Finish	Long and round with the smokiness to the end
Flavour	Smokey, dry with a touch of sweetness, slightly woody
Water	Crosshill Loch and a spring on the premises
History	

Geography Longrow is a still within the building which houses and is known as Springbank Distillery.

Notes Although the current brand was only introduced in 1973, the name was established in 1874. The old Longrow distillery is now Springbank's car park!

The Macallan

Established	1824
Age/Strength	10 years 40% abv
Distillery	Macallan
Address	Craigellachie, Morayshire
Map reference	NJ277444

Colour	Richly golden
Nose	Delightful, rich and sherried sweet
Finish	Long and lingering
Flavour	Smooth, sweet, full, rich
Water	The Ringorm Burn
History	Until the bridge at Craigellachie was built by Thomas Telford in 1814, the ford across the Spey at Macallan was one of the few on the river. It was much used by cattle drovers, and whisky distilled at the old farm distillery which preceded the licensed distillery was a popular feature of the river crossing for them. The distillery, although now a public limited company, was until quite recently controlled by the successors of Robert Kemp who had purchased it in 1892. Even today they are still very much involved in the business. The distillery was extended in the early 1950s and again in 1959, but the demand for Macallan fillings has been such that it was doubled from six to 12 stills in 1965 and increased to 18 in 1974 and 21 in 1975.
Geography	On a hillside overlooking the Spey with the old Easter Elchies farmhouse (it was originally a farm distillery) now magnificently refurbished as corporate offices.

Notes	The makers of Macallan have championed the use of sherry casks for maturing whisky, and have helped to reverse the trend away from their use. All of Macallan's output is now aged in sherry casks, following extensive research into the results obtained from various types of sherry wood and other casks.

The Macallan

Age/Strength 18 years old (1967 distillation). 43% abv

Colour Rich, golden, deeper than the 10-year old
Nose Rich, sherry-sweet, oaky-oily vanilla
Finish Long, sweet, very distinguished
Flavour Sweet, round rich, velvety smooth, less spirity than the 10-year old

The Macallan

Age/Strength 25 years 43% abv

Colour Deep oaky amber, lovely gold highlights
Nose Full, rich, nutty, sherry-sweetness
Finish Long, dry, lightly spicy, nutty
Flavour Big, rich, medium-sweet, creamy, oaky, velvety-smooth, but woody

Notes Special and celebratory bottles of Macallan of even greater age can occasionally be obtained.

Mannochmore

Established	1971
Age/Strength	Not currently available
Distillery	Mannochmore
Address	By Elgin, Morayshire
Map reference	NJ 213573

Colour	
Nose	
Finish	
Flavour	
Water	The Bardon Burn
History	Built by SMD and licensed to John Haig & Co. Mannochmore was built on the same 25-acre (10 hectares) site as the older Glenlossie distillery (1876). Mannochmore does not utilise the purifier between the lyne arm and the condenser which Glenlossie does. Part of United Distillers plc.
Geography	Sited next to Glenlossie at Thornshill on an unclassified road to the west of the A941, two miles south of Elgin.

Notes	Mothballed in 1985, Mannochmore is now producing once again (October 1988) — a sure sign of the health of the industry. Very rarely available as a single malt.

Millburn

Established	1807
Age/Strength	1966 distillation 40% abv
Distillery	Millburn
Address	Inverness
Map reference	NH 679457

Colour	Deep syrupy golden
Nose	Woody, slightly spirity, dryish
Finish	A little flat spot then finishes well, dry finish
Flavour	Round, slightly woody with a touch of fruit, medium-sweet
Water	Loch Duntelchaig
History	Said to have been founded by a Mr Welsh. The earliest recorded reference held by United Distillers dates from 1825, when James Rose and Alex MacDonald were named as the licence holders. Probably used as a corn mill in the mid-1800s. Rebuilt 1876. Was owned by Booth's, the gin distillers, from 1921 to 1937. Bought by SMD in 1943. There were two stills.
Geography	Millburn was located about one mile east of the centre of Inverness on the banks of the stream from which it took its name.

Notes	Fire broke out on 26 April 1922, but the local fire brigade, "greatly assisted" by the Cameron Highlanders, saved the stillhouse and storage warehouses. The commander of the 3rd Battalion, Lt. Col. David Price Haig, had owned the distillery until 1921. The distillery was closed during the Second World War and used as a billet for troops. The distillery was knocked down when sold for property development in 1988, a fate which befell all three remaining Inverness distilleries during that year. Gordon & MacPhail bottling.

Milton Duff

Established	1824
Age/Strength	12 years 40% abv
Distillery	Miltonduff
Address	Near Elgin, Morayshire
Map reference	NJ 183602

Colour	Straw/golden with greenish edges
Nose	Medium to full, fragrant, slightly floral, sweet
Finish	Almost delicate, refined and long
Flavour	Sweet, fruity, full and round
Water	Reputedly the Black Burn
History	The distillery is said to have been founded by Pearey and Bain. It came into the ownership of Hiram Walker in 1936 and is now part of the Allied Lyons group of companies. The distillery was extended in the mid-1890s and was largely rebuilt in 1974-75. Licensed to George Ballantine & Son Ltd.
Geography	On the west of the B9010 to the south of Elgin. A short distance away across the River Lossie are the ruins of Pluscarden Priory.

Notes	In the years of the 18th and early 19th centuries, the waters of the Black Burn supplied scores of small illicit stills in the Glen of Pluscarden, the fertile barley-rich plain being ideal for their situation. Milton Duff is the principal malt associated with Ballantine's blended Scotch whisky.

Mortlach

Established	1823
Age/Strength	22 years (bottled at 46% abv.)
Distillery	Mortlach
Address	Dufftown, Banffshire
Map reference	NF 328398

Colour	Gold/amber, good yellow highlights
Nose	Sweet, creamy, slightly coconut, oaky
Finish	Cold, slightly spicy and oaky
Flavour	Sweet, woody, possibly a bit old
Water	Springs in the Conval Hills
History	The first of Dufftown's "seven stills". It was owned for a time by Messrs J. & J. Grant of Glen Grant and was then unoccupied for some years, the barley granary serving as a free church until one was erected. Extended from three to six stills in 1897. Acquired by John Walker & Sons in 1923, by which time it was the largest distillery in the area. Passed to the DCL in 1925 and transferred to SMD to operate in 1930. The old Mortlach was somewhat cramped and was demolished and rebuilt in the early 1960s, re-opening in 1964. Now part of United Distillers plc.
Geography	Sited at the junction of the A941 and B9014 on the eastern outskirts of Dufftown.

Notes	In the hollow in which the distillery lies (Mortlach means bowl-shaped valley) was fought the battle, in 1010, at which the Scottish King Malcolm II defeated the Danes. Tradition has it that the distillery is also on the site of an illicit still which drew its water from a spring called Highland John's Well. Unlike most malt distilleries, Mortlach had permission to stay open during the Second World War, except in 1944. Wm Cadenhead bottling.

North Port

Established	1820
Age/Strength	1970 distillation
Distillery	North Port
Address	Brechin, Angus
Map reference	NO 598607

Colour	Gold with yellow highlights
Nose	Sweet, heather honey, rich
Finish	Slightly astringent strangely, but lasts well
Flavour	Medium-sweet, full, round
Water	Loch Lee — the town water supply
History	It originally traded as Townhead Distillery, changing to Brechin Distillery in 1823 and North Port in 1839. Run by SMD since 1922 and silent 1928-37. Two stills.
Geography	Sited north west of the city centre of Brechin.

Notes	The distillery takes its name from the North Gate in the ancient city walls, long since vanished. North Port would seem to have been something of a nepotistic society; fathers and sons worked together for long periods, and there was little chance of a vacant job unless there was a death. Closed. Gordon & MacPhail bottling.

Oban

Established	1794
Age/Strength	14 years 43% abv
Distillery	Oban
Address	Stafford Street, Oban, Argyllshire
Map reference	NM 859302

Colour	Very pale straw with gold highlights
Nose	Medium-sweet, lightly peated, quite rich, slight burnt heather.
Finish	Smokey, dry and delicate.
Flavour	Smooth, lightly sweet, creamy, very delicate peatiness.
Water	Two lochs in Ardconnel, one mile above the town.
History	The distillery was built by the Stevenson family who also founded the town of Oban, which was previously just a small fishing village. Rebuilt c 1884. Became part of the DCL in 1925 and has been operated by SMD since 1930. The stillhouse was rebuilt 1969-72. Two stills. Now part of United Distillers plc.
Geography	Situated in the centre and built before most of the town.

Notes	Nose and flavour are reminiscent of Bowmore although more subtle and delicate. This is a new introduction, one of the United Distillers' Classic Malts portfolio.

Oban

Age/Strength	12 years 40% abv

Colour	Fairly dark amber with an apparent syrupy texture
Nose	Clean, slightly spirity with a delicate peaty/heather aroma
Finish	Good length and a smokey aftertaste
Flavour	Very smooth, slightly peppery with hints of heather

Old Fettercairn

Established	1824
Age/Strength	10 years 40% abv
Distillery	Fettercairn
Address	Fettercairn, Kincardineshire
Map reference	NO 645737

Colour	Straw with good gold highlights
Nose	Quite full, dryish, vanilla oak, malty
Finish	Dry, long and chewy
Flavour	Dry, spicy, medium weight, creamy smooth
Water	Springs in the nearby Cairngorm mountains
History	The distillery originally stood two miles higher up the mountain in the heart of a smuggling district, but this was abandoned in 1824 when the present works were opened. Rebuilt in 1887-90 after a fire. Extended from two to four stills in 1966. Now owned by Whyte & Mackay.
Geography	Situated close to the River Esk on the outskirts of Fettercairn off the B974, the distillery rests at the foot of the Cairngorm mountains.

Notes	In 1829, one John Gladstone bought the nearby Fasque estate. He was the father of William Ewart Gladstone, one of Britain's most illustrious prime ministers, and probably the best friend the whisky industry ever had among their number. He introduced several reforms crucial to the industry, the most important of which was in 1853 when he abolished the crippling malt tax. Another was to permit the sale of bottled whisky to the public.

Old Pulteney

Established	1826
Age/Strength	8 years 40% abv
Distillery	Pulteney
Address	Wick, Caithness
Map reference	ND 368501

Colour	Palish gold with tinges of green
Nose	Delicately pungent, faint tangs of ozone
Finish	Smokey, dry, refreshing
Flavour	Quite pungent, smokey, clean
Water	The Loch of Hempriggs
History	Established by one James Henderson. Became part of the DCL in 1925, having been purchased by John Dewar & Sons a couple of years earlier. Closed between 1930 and 1951, when revived. In 1955 it was bought by Hiram Walker, now part of Allied Lyons, who rebuilt the distillery in 1959. Two stills.
Geography	The furthest north distillery on the UK mainland. It is sited on the southern side of Wick, close to the North Sea coast.

Notes	Only available from the independent bottlers, in this case, Gordon and McPhail. It is reputed to be one of the fastest maturing of malt whiskies. One of the main malts associated with Ballantine's blended Scotch whisky.

Pittyvaich

Established	1975
Age/Strength	Not available as a single
Distillery	Pittyvaich
Address	Dufftown, Banffshire
Map reference	NJ 323390

Colour	
Nose	
Finish	
Flavour	
Water	The distillery draws its mashing water from two springs, Convalleys and Balliemore.
History	Built by Arthur Bell & Sons Ltd as a sister to Dufftown and operated in conjunction with it. Four stills. Now part of United Distillers plc.
Geography	Situated in the Dullan Glen on the outskirts of Dufftown near the 6th century Mortlach parish church. Part of the Dufftown complex.

Notes	The make uses the same water source as Dufftown and gives a similar whisky.

Port Ellen

Established	1825
Age/Strength	1970 distillation 40% abv
Distillery	Port Ellen
Address	Port Ellen, Islay
Map reference	NR 358458

Colour	Peaty/gold with bright highlights
Nose	Big, pungent, peaty, slightly rubbery, dry
Finish	Long, pungent and smokey
Flavour	Big, burnt peat, an edge of sweetness, very distinctive
Water	Two local lochs
History	Founded by A.K. Mackay & Co. Acquired by John Ramsay and run by him and his heirs until 1920. Bought by the DCL in 1927 and transferred to SMD in 1930. Silent 1929 to 1966, although the maltings continued in use. The distillery was extensively rebuilt in 1967, when increased from two to four stills. A large new maltings was erected in 1973. The distillery ceased production again in May 1983, although the maltings now serves all the Islay distilleries following an historic agreement between the producing companies in 1987.
Geography	Situated about half a mile from Port Ellen, the maltings building now dominates the shoreline.

Notes	The Excise Act of 1824 enforced the introduction of the spirit safe in distilleries. Tests had to be made to ensure that it had no harmful effect on the make. The official experiments were carried out in Port Ellen. The maltings were visited by Her Majesty Queen Elizabeth II on 11 August 1980. Gordon & MacPhail bottling.

Rosebank

Established	1840
Age/Strength	12 years 40% abv
Distillery	Rosebank
Address	Falkirk, Stirlingshire
Map reference	NS 876803

Colour	Palish gold/amber with green tinges
Nose	Light, spirity, astringent
Finish	Quite good length, somewhat fiery
Flavour	Dry, a little spirity, spicy
Water	Carron Valley Reservoir
History	The distillery, established by James Rankine, is said to have been converted from the maltings of the earlier Camelon distillery. Rebuilt in 1864. In 1914 the Rosebank Distillery Ltd, as it was then called, was one of the companies merged into the formation of Scottish Malt Distillers Ltd. Now part of United Distillers plc.
Geography	Sited on the banks of the Forth and Clyde canal where the A803 intersects with the canal on the north side of Falkirk.

Notes	The make is triple distilled.

Royal Brackla

Established	1812
Age/Strength	18 years 46% vol
Distillery	Royal Brackla
Address	Nairn
Map reference	NH 862515

Colour	Pale straw, good yellow highlights, definite green tinge
Nose	Round, sweet and fruity
Finish	Velvety smooth, long and distinguished
Flavour	Sweet, smooth, round, rich
Water	The Cawdor Burn
History	Said to have been founded by Captain William Fraser. Purchased by SMD in 1943. Rebuilt 1965-6 and extended from two to four stills in 1970.
Geography	Sited to the north west of the B9090, 1Å miles south of Nairn.

Notes	Brackla was the first distillery to be granted a Royal warrant in 1835. It was referred to at that time as "Brackla" or "The King's Own Whisky". A native of Nairn, James Augustus Grant, accompanied Captain Speke on his last journey to discover the source of the Nile. Brackla comforted them "in that most dreaded of countries, Africa". In days long gone, illicit stills could be found in abundance here on the banks of the Cawdor Burn. Some of the older buildings were converted to a visitor centre in 1982/3, it being three quarters of a mile from Cawdor Castle, Wm Cadenhead bottling.

Royal Lochnagar

Established	1845
Age/Strength	12 years 40% abv
Distillery	Royal Lochnagar
Address	Crathie, Ballater, Aberdeenshire
Map reference	NO 267938

Colour	Pale straw, bright gold highlights
Nose	Pleasant, slightly peppery and fruity
Finish	Good smooth length
Flavour	Sweet, clean, creamy, slightly peppery
Water	Springs in the foothills of Lochnagar
History	Originally known as 'New Lochnagar', as another Lochnagar distillery had been built nearby in 1826. It obtained the Royal Warrant after its owner, John Begg, had invited Queen Victoria and Prince Albert to the distillery in 1848 to taste some of the malt. The buildings were rebuilt in 1906. Two stills. Now part of United Distillers plc.
Geography	The only remaining distillery on Deeside. It overlooks Balmoral Castle.

Notes	Close to the royal residence of Balmoral, Royal Lochnagar has a very popular visitors' centre, converted in 1987 from old distillery buildings.

Royal Lochnagar Selected Reserve

Age/Strength	No age statement. 43% abv

Colour	Deep peaty amber with good gold highlights
Nose	Rich, wet oak, vanilla, sweet, lightly sherried
Finish	Long, slightly spicy and very smooth
Flavour	Full, round, rich and mellow, nutty and creamy

St Magdalene

Established	c 1795
Age/Strength	Sample not available
Distillery	St Magdalene
Address	Linlithgow, West Lothian
Map reference	NT 008771

Colour	
Nose	
Finish	
Flavour	
Water	The town's domestic supply, which comes from Loch Lomond
History	Said to have been founded by Sebastian Henderson in the 18th century at St Magdalene's Cross. The former site of an annual fair and of St Magdalene's Hospital, St Magdalene was one of the five distilleries which originated Scottish Malt Distillers in July 1914.
Geography	Sited at the eastern end of Linlithgow where the railway line, running alongside the Union Canal, intersects with the A706.
Notes	Linlithgow was a centre of milling and malting in the 17th century and of brewing and distilling in the 18th. The distillery is now closed and part is being developed for housing.

Scapa

Established	1885
Age/Strength	8 years 57% abv
Distillery	Scapa
Address	Kirkwall, Orkney
Map reference	HY 434089

Colour	Peaty/amber with good gold highlights and a greenish tinge
Nose	Spirity, somewhat astringent, peaty
Finish	Good, spicy and long-lived
Flavour	Sweet, rich, full, lightly oaky, malty
Water	The Lingro Burn and nearby springs
History	Built by Macfarlane & Townsend. Owned by Hiram Walker (now part of Allied Lyons) since 1954. The wash still was replaced by a "Lomond" still in 1959, this producing a heavier spirit than longer necked stills.
Geography	Sited on the Lingro Burn two miles south west of Kirkwall on the A964 at the head of Scapa Bay.

Notes	For a malt with such a pronounced astringent nose, the palate is surprisingly sweet. Scapa Flow was where the German fleet was scuttled at the end of World War I. One of the main malts associated with Ballantine's blended Scotch whisky. Gordon & MacPhail bottling.

The Singleton of Auchroisk

S

Established	1974
Age/Strength	12 years 40% abv
Distillery	Auchroisk
Address	Mulben, Banffshire
Map reference	NJ 350512

Colour	Fairly peaty golden, quite dark syrupy
Nose	Sweet, peaches, full, almost minty, slightly damp
Finish	Long and smooth — a distinguished whisky
Flavour	Sweet, full and round, smokey, smooth and very mellow
Water	Dorie's Well
History	Managed by IDV, who are part of Grand Metropolitan. Eight stills.
Geography	On the north side of the A95 between Keith and Aberlour.

Notes   A new distillery producing its first make in 1975. Despite being new, the buildings are well designed and blend in well with the surroundings. Sherry casks are used predominantly. Auchroisk is a showpiece distillery and has an old steam engine from Strathmill preserved in its entrance hall.

Speyburn

Established	1897
Age/Strength	1971 distillation 40% abv
Distillery	Speyburn
Address	Rothes, Morayshire
Map reference	NJ 273503

Colour	Rich, peaty/amber with good gold highlights
Nose	Sweet, fruity, slightly spirity
Finish	Mellow, reasonable length with oak on the end
Flavour	Medium-sweet, lightish, smooth
Water	The Granty (or Birchfield) Burn
History	Built by the Speyburn-Glenlivet Distillery Co Ltd. Became part of DCL in 1916. Transferred to SMD in 1962. It was the first malt distillery to instal a drum maltings, which closed in 1968. Two stills. Now part of United Distillers plc.
Geography	Situated on an unclassified road, the old road from Rothes to Elgin, a quarter of a mile north west of the B9015 on the northern outskirts of Rothes. The buildings were constructed in a compact style because "the hilly nature of the ground" required height rather than breadth. The main block and warehouses are therefore unusually two storeys high.

Notes	Speyburn started up in the last week of December 1897. Doors and windows still had not been fitted to the stillhouse and, as a severe snowstorm was sweeping the district, employees had to work in overcoats. Just one butt of spirit was bonded with 1897 on its head. Speyburn was another distillery used as a billet for troops between 1940 and 1944. Gordon & MacPhail bottling.

Springbank

Established	1828
Age/Strength	10 years 46% abv
Distillery	Springbank
Address	Campbeltown, Ayrshire
Map reference	NR 718205

Colour	Pale straw, yellow highlights
Nose	Lightish, sweetish, slight hints of coconut oil
Finish	Good, smooth and distinctive
Flavour	Sweet, smooth, creamy, slight hint of coconut
Water	Crosshill Loch
History	Said to have been originally licensed to the Reid family. It was acquired by John and William Mitchell in 1837 and passed through various family hands until 1897 when the present owning company, J & A Mitchell & Co, was incorporated. Three stills.
Geography	The distillery is in the centre of the town.

Notes	The Campbeltown area once boasted around 30 distilleries. Springbank is now one of only two survivors. One of only three single malts still to be bottled at the distillery itself. The others are Glenfiddich and Lochside.

Springbank

Age/Strength	21 years 46% abv

Colour	Deep amber
Nose	Definite fruity notes, stickily sweet in their richness, also floral notes and a suggestion of coconut
Finish	Very fine and long
Flavour	Silkily smooth, full bodied and creamy

Strathisla

Established	1786
Age/Strength	12 years
Distillery	Strathisla
Address	Keith, Banffshire
Map reference	NJ 429511

Colour	Bright gold/straw
Nose	Full, sweet, fruity, appley, very pronounced and rich
Finish	Long, fine and mellow
Flavour	Rich, warm, quite full, sweet
Water	The Broomhill Spring
History	Built as Milltown (Keith was the centre of the Scottish linen industry), and later known as Milton, Strathisla was originally the name of the make and subsequently became that of the distillery as well. The distillery was twice badly damaged in the 1870s, first by fire in 1876, and three years later as the result of an explosion. Extensive modernisation took place after these events and again in 1965, when the distillery was enlarged from two to six stills. It is today owned by Chivas Brothers Ltd, a subsidiary of The Seagram Company of Canada.
Geography	Half a mile from the centre of Keith.

Notes	The reservoir where the water supply is collected is said to be visited nightly by "the water kelpies" which could account for its special flavour. Gordon & MacPhail bottling.

Strathisla

Age/Strength	8 years 40% abv

Colour	Amber with good gold highlights
Nose	Fruity, spirity, sweet lanolin oiliness
Finish	Fair body, perhaps a little short
Flavour	Spicy, medium-sweet, touch of oak, quite smooth

Strathmill

S

Established	1891
Age/Strength	Sample not available
Distillery	Strathmill
Address	Keith, Banffshire
Map reference	NJ 425502

Colour	
Nose	
Finish	
Flavour	
Water	A spring at the distillery
History	Originally a corn and flour mill, it was converted in 1891 as Glenisla-Glenlivet. Acquired by W & A Gilbey in 1895, when it was renamed Strathmill. Became part of IDV in 1962 and now absorbed into Grand Metropolitan. Doubled from two to four stills in late 1960s. The Distillery is operated by Justerini & Brooks (Scotland) Ltd.
Geography	Sited within 100 yards of the turning on to the B9014 from Keith to Dufftown.

Notes	Very rarely available as a single, the make largely goes into the J & B blend.

Talisker

Established	1831
Age/Strength	10 years 45.8% abv
Distillery	Talisker
Address	Carbost, Isle of Skye
Map reference	NG 377318

Colour	Straw with gold highlights
Nose	Pungent, peaty, burnt heather, hints of ozone
Finish	Smokey, spicy, smooth, almost salty at the end
Flavour	Peaty, dry, spicy, quite creamy
Water	From the Carbost Burn on the slopes of Cnoc Nan Speireag (Stockveil Hill)
History	The distillery was originally sited at Snizort, to the north of the island, but closed and mysteriously moved. Founded by Hugh and Kenneth MacAskill. Rebuilt 1880-87 and extended in 1900. Merged into Dailuaine-Talisker Distilleries in 1898, under which name it still trades although absorbed fully into the DCL in 1925. Operated by SMD. Rebuilt in 1960 after a stillhouse fire. Five stills.
Geography	Situated in a gentle bowl which forms a lonely, very sheltered glen on the west coast of Skye.

Notes	The only distillery on the island of Skye, it took its name from a farm about six miles distant. The make was triple distilled until 1928. This is a new introduction, one of the United Distillers' Classic Malts.

Talisker

Age/Strength	8 years 40% abv

Colour	Lovely amber with green highlights
Nose	Pungent, full and peaty, but soft
Finish	Long with a burst of flavour on swallowing
Flavour	Dry, spicy, full, with a lot of smokiness

Tamdhu

Established	1897
Age/Strength	10 years 40% abv
Distillery	Tamdhu
Address	Knockando, Morayshire
Map reference	NJ 189418

Colour	Pale golden, amber highlights
Nose	Lightish with a hint of sweetness akin to apples
Finish	Soft, creamily smooth and smokey
Flavour	Round, mellow, sweet and slightly spicy and peaty
Water	A sping under the distillery
History	Built by the Tamdhu Distillery Co. Ltd which was owned by a consortium of blenders. Owned by Highland Distilleries Co. since 1898. Closed from 1927-47 but extended in 1972 from two to four stills and again to six in 1975. A feature is its Saladin Maltings, largely rebuilt.
Geography	Sited on the banks of the River Spey south of the B9102 between Knockando and Archiestown.

Notes	The old railway station at Knockando has been converted into a visitor centre for Tamdhu. Tamdhu does not have the traditional pagoda heads atop its kilns, having instead a short, square concrete chimney. The only distillery to malt all its own barley on site.

Tamnavulin

Established	1966
Age/Strength	10 years 40% abv
Distillery	Tamnavulin
Address	Tomnavoulin, Banffshire
Map reference	NJ 213260

Colour	Very pale straw with golden highlights
Nose	Light, sweet with a slightly floral edge
Finish	Long, easy and slightly spicy
Flavour	Mature, sweet, light, gently oaky
Water	Subterranean springs at Easterton in the local hills
History	Built by the Tamnavulin-Glenlivet Distillery Co., a subsidiary of Invergordon Distillers. Six stills. A very modern distillery, it can be operated by just a handful of technicians.
Geography	Sited on the east side of the B9008 at the village of Tomnavoulin.

Notes	The only distillery actually positioned on the river Livet, from which cooling and other process waters are drawn. Tomnavoulin in Gaelic means "mill on the hill", and an old carding mill which stands on the river just below the distillery has been converted into a very attractive visitors' centre. The mill machinery has been preserved inside. Equally pleasant are the grassy banks of the river which have been turned into a picnic area. Tamnavulin is naturally light in colour, taking any colour it has from the casks in which it is matured, no caramel being added to the make.

Teaninich

Established	1817
Age/Strength	Sample not available
Distillery	Teaninich
Address	Alness, Ross-shire
Map reference	NH 653691

Colour	
Nose	
Finish	
Flavour	
Water	Dairywell Spring
History	Founded by Captain Hugo Munro. An entirely new distillation unit named "A side" began production in 1970. "B side", the milling, mashing and fermentation part of the old distillery was rebuilt in 1973. Ten stills. Now owned by United Distillers plc.
Geography	Sited to the south of the A9 on the western outskirts of Alness and on the west bank of the River Alness, three quarters of a mile from its outlet into the Cromarty Firth.

Notes	Barnard recorded in 1887 that Teaninich was the only distillery north of Inverness to be "lighted by electricity". In 1925 both malting floors were of solid clay. Closed.

Tobermory

Established	1798
Age/Strength	Age not stated 40% abv
Distillery	Tobermory
Address	Tobermory, Isle of Mull
Map reference	NM 504551

Colour	Pale golden
Nose	Fruity, fairly light
Finish	Finishes smokily and rather woody
Flavour	Soft, well balanced, smooth, slightly sweet edge
Water	Misnish Lochs
History	Established by one John Sinclair. Taken over by DCL in 1916. Silent 1930-72. Now owned by a Yorkshire-based property company. Four stills.
Geography	Sited at the head of Tobermory Bay.

Notes The only distillery on Mull. The distillery was also known as "Ledaig" until 1978 when it was renamed Tobermory. It has also been referred to as "Mull". Bottlings of the malt can be found under the name of Ledaig. The distillery re-opened in 1990 after extensive modernisation. It now offers a visitors facility. Because of a shortage of fillings Tobermory is a vatted malt. However it is expected that more single malt will be available in due course.

Tomatin

Established	1897
Age/Strength	10 years 43% abv
Distillery	Tomatin
Address	Tomatin, Inverness-shire
Map reference	NH 790295

Colour	Straw with yellowy gold highlights
Nose	Dryish, malty, leafy, spirity with a sweet edge
Finish	Spicy, lightly peaty, slightly grapey
Flavour	Medium-sweet, smooth, soft, round, slightly smokey
Water	Alt-Na-Frithe (a local burn)
History	Founded by the Tomatin Spey District Distillery Co. Ltd. Extended from two to four stills in 1956, to six in 1958, to 10 in 1961, to 11 in 1964 and finally to 23 in 1974.
Geography	Sited on the west of the A9 at the village of Tomatin, 12 miles south of Inverness. At 1,028 feet above sea level it is one of Scotland's highest distilleries.

Notes	The first distillery to be owned by a Japanese company and with the potential for the highest output (more than 12 million litres of alcohol) of all the malt distilleries. In Gaelic Tomatin means "the hill of bushes". Bottled by Tomatin Distillery Co.

Tomintoul

Established	1964
Age/Strength	12 years 40% abv
Distillery	Tomintoul
Address	Near Tomintoul, Banffshire
Map reference	NJ 149254

Colour	Peaty straw with good gold highlights
Nose	Medium-sweet, rich, spirity, vanilla, fruity — almost orangey
Finish	Spirity, spicy, quite smooth, the oaky flavour lingers
Flavour	Medium-sweet, lightish, slightly peppery, oaky
Water	The Ballantruan Spring
History	A modern distillery, production only began in 1965 and it was not until 1972 that the make began to appear in bottle. Built by the Tomintoul Distillery Ltd and bought by Scottish & Universal Investment Trust (part of Lonrho) in 1973. Managed by Whyte & Mackay, who were bought from Lonrho by Brent Walker towards the end of 1988. Doubled from two to four stills in 1974.
Geography	Situated in the valley of the River Avon on the A939 Grantown-on-Spey to Bridge of Avon road.

Notes	Tomintoul is the highest village in the Scottish Highlands although the distillery itself is not quite as high above sea level as Dalwhinnie. Tomintoul is regularly cut off by snow in winter. The third Highland malt distillery to be built since the Second World War and the first to be built and financed by Scottish capital on Speyside this century.

Tormore

Established	1958
Age/Strength	10 years 40% abv
Distillery	Tormore
Address	Advie, Grantown-on-Spey, Morayshire
Map reference	NJ 154350

Colour	Pale golden
Nose	Light, delicate, sometimes described as flinty; unusual dryness
Finish	Fine, distinguished and long
Flavour	Slightly sweet, of medium weight and slightly spirity
Water	The Achvochkie Burn
History	Built 1958-60 by Long John Distillers Ltd, now part of James Burrough Distillers (parent company Whitbread). Doubled from four to eight stills in 1972.
Geography	South of the A95 between Grantown-on-Spey and the Bridge of Avon.

Notes The first new Highland malt distillery to be built in the 20th century. The distillery and associated housing are of most striking design, the work of Sir Albert Richardson, a past president of the Royal Academy.

Tullibardine

Established	1949
Age/Strength	10 years 40% abv
Distillery	Tullibardine
Address	Blackford, Perthshire
Map reference	NN 896087

Colour	Straw, goldy-green highlights
Nose	Quite full, soft, malty and earthy
Finish	Peppery, warm and quite long, slightly bitter at the end
Flavour	Dryish, spicy, with a richness and roundness, quite smooth
Water	The Danny Burn
History	There was a previous Tullibardine distillery near Blackford which was established in 1798, although its exact location is not known. The new distillery was the work of Delme Evans, who also established Jura and Glenallachie. Owned by Invergordon Distillers since 1971. Rebuilt in 1973-4 and enlarged from two to four stills.
Geography	Situated south of the A9 on the south western outskirts of the village of Blackford, four miles south west of Auchterarder.

Notes	On the site of an ancient brewery, the distillery takes its name from the nearby Tullibardine Moor, home of Gleneagles Hotel and golf courses. This area has always been famed for its water, e.g. Highland Spring is from Blackford. Tradition has it that the fair Queen Helen of Scotland was drowned at a ford on the Allan River, hence the name Blackford.

and one for the future . . .

Established	1989
Distillery	Speyside
Address	Kingussie

History

A new distillery that is yet to go on stream. It is situated on the banks of the River Tromie opposite the site of the of the old Speyside distillery which closed circa 1911. The distillery is on land which was purchased by its owners, the Christie family, in 1956, together with stretches of the Spey and Tromie rivers. Building did not begin until 1969 and was finished in 1985 but the plant is not yet complete.

Geography

On the banks of the River Tromie, close by its confluence with the River Spey

Notes

The owners say that the new distillery will have a maximum capacity of 200,000 gallons a year, although it is only intended to produce between 50-100,000 gallons, all of which will be kept for their own use. It will be some years before the new make is available as a single malt, however, although the owners do presently market a vatted malt under the name Speyside. The distillery's founder, George Christie, lives in the house previously owned by G.McPherson Grant who, as well as building the original Speyside distillery, also built Tomatin and Newtonmore. Only Tomatin of this original trio still exists.

Do you know your Ardmore from your elbow? Can you tell a Cardhu from a Caperdonich?

If not and you've enjoyed this book, why not fill in the coupon overleaf for full details of Malt Whisky Association membership and special offers. (You can photocopy the page or simply write requesting the information you require if you don't want to spoil your book).

The Malt Whisky Association was formed to promote the appreciaton and enjoyment of single malt whisky. It is completely indepedent of the whisky producers and suppliers. Benefits include:

- *The Malt Letter*, a quality members only publication.
- Membership discounts and privileges
- Special member prices on the comprehensive "Master of Malt" selection of single malt whiskies. More than 200 different malts and ages are available in bottle and miniature.
- A wide selection of special offers including publications and gift items.

In addition, you can conduct your own 'blind' tasting with the unique Master of Malt Nosing Selection.

If you enclose £2 to cover our post and packing costs, we will also send you a free introductory copy of *The Malt Letter*

NB All requests from outside UK should include £3 or US $5.

To: The Malt Whisky Association, Freepost, Largs, Ayrshire, Scotland KA30 8BR

Please print clearly

○ I would like membership details

○ I would like details of publications, gift selections, special offers and miniatures

○ I would like a copy of the "Master of Malt" list of mail order single malt whiskies

○ I would like an introductory copy of The Malt Letter and enclose £2 towards post and packing (£3 or US $5 or equivalent in cash or credit card payment instructions for all enquiries outside UK)

Name ————————————————————————

Address ————————————————————————

————————————————————————

Town ————————————————————————

Postcode ————————————————————————

Country ————————————————————————